TEACHER'S RESOURCE MANUAL

Exercises in Critical Thinking

Thinking
······It······
Through

CHANGES

GLOBE FEARON
EDUCATIONAL PUBLISHER
PARAMUS, NEW JERSEY

Paramount Publishing

Executive Editor: Barbara Levadi
Editor: Carol Schneider
Editorial Assistant: Roger Weisman
Critical Thinking Consultants: Sandra Parks and Ruth Townsend
Teacher Consultants: Eunice Grippaldi and Carol Sumner
Product Development: Maggie Pruce
Art Director: Nancy Sharkey
Designer: Joan Jacobus
Production Director: Penny Gibson
Manufacturing Supervisor: Della Smith
Senior Production Editor: Linda Greenberg
Production Editor: Alan Dalgleish
Marketing Manager: Sandra Hutchison
Electronic Page Production: Impressions
Cover Design: Design Five

Printed in the United States of America 1 2 3 4 5 6 7 8 9 10 99 98 97 96 95 94

ISBN: 0-835–90930–1

GLOBE FEARON
EDUCATIONAL PUBLISHER
PARAMUS, NEW JERSEY

Paramount Publishing

CONTENTS

Program Philosophy and Rationale

What Is Critical Thinking?

Certainly no one today would doubt the importance of good thinking in surviving in today's society. But what exactly is thinking? And what constitutes good thinking?

According to many educational theorists, there are three types of higher-order thinking: creative, analytical, and critical thinking. Critical thinking may be the most inclusive and the most rigorous, as it requires the analysis of any idea or belief in order to judge its validity or worth. Critical thinking, therefore, is evaluative thinking. It includes, among other skills, the ability to:

- ascertain the reliability of ideas or sources of information
- verify the factual accuracy of statements
- distinguish facts from opinions or suggestions
- detect bias or lack of objectivity
- weigh and prioritize the strength of ideas or arguments

In his taxonomy, Benjamin Bloom identified and then ordered six categories of thinking from least to most rigorous: *knowing, comprehending, applying, analyzing, synthesizing,* and *evaluating.* All are important and necessary. Simple recall or identification, is "knowing," or the lowest level of thinking. Critical thinking, or "evaluation," is the highest order. It is also the most inclusive, since it requires the application of all other categories. According to Bloom and many other theorists, all lower- and higher-order processes and skills lead to critical thinking. They are necessary steps toward reaching the ultimate goal of being able to think critically.

Critical Thinking in Language Arts Instruction

Thinking It Through was developed to help language arts teachers incorporate critical thinking into their curriculum. The program supplements topics and skills that language arts teachers are already teaching. The goal of this program is to provide instruction and practice in the processes that will lead students to become independent critical thinkers.

Thinking It Through is appropriate for students of all ability levels and backgrounds. The *Teacher's Resource Manual* (TRM) offers useful suggestions and procedures for helping all students to improve their thinking.

Each unit in *Thinking It Through* focuses on a topic that is interesting and relevant to students' lives. The topics provide the context for exercising students' higher-order and critical thinking skills through a step-by-step process. By using, rather than teaching, content, the units in *Thinking It Through* focus on thinking skills related to language arts.

Each unit begins with a thought-provoking selection (a short story, playlet, news article, questionnaire) that initiates the thinking process. The selections activate students' prior knowledge about the topics and stimulate students to begin thinking and talking about the issues. For example, in one short story students see fallacious reasoning and characters that aren't thinking critically. The questionnaires require students to evaluate information and to make decisions.

The Language of Thinking

Each unit also contains three or four lessons. Each lesson concentrates on one important thinking skill. As students do the lesson activities, they learn and practice the process and language of thinking. The lesson activities, as well as the project at the end of each unit, call for students to be actively involved. Many lessons include a discussion feature that provides provocative and controversial questions that require students to apply higher-order thinking to real-life issues and problems.

The activities and projects employ a variety of graphic formats. The graphic organizers help students to record, display, arrange, categorize, and visualize ideas. They encourage organized thinking and represent formats that students can use in other subject areas. The graphic organizers appeal to students with differing learning styles and ability levels.

Many activities in *Thinking It Through* encourage students to weigh and debate issues and to describe their thinking processes and strategies. In addition, Thinking Journal activities in the TRM prompt students to record the critical thinking strategies they use and encourage students to use these same strategies in other subject areas and in their daily lives. As students become more proficient at describing their metacognitive processes, they also become more adept at using the language of thinking.

The lessons include opportunities for students to assess their performance. Students are provided with several questions that require them to reflect upon their thinking and the processes they employed. Many of the self-evaluation questions can become the basis for Thinking Journal entries.

The projects at the end of each unit give students an opportunity to synthesize information and to apply skills in a final product or presentation. Projects also serve as a means for assessing and evaluating students' growth in higher-order and critical thinking.

Thinking It Through, with its variety of activity formats and interesting content, is a program with a strong dual purpose: to help prepare students to become critical, independent thinkers in today's complex society, and to encourage teenagers to articulate their ideas clearly and logically.

Why Teach Critical Thinking?

In 1984, The National Commission on Excellence in Education's *A Nation At Risk* (1984) lamented students' inability to think creatively, analytically, and evaluatively. It encouraged educators to infuse critical thinking skills into their school curricula. Since that report, other studies and organizations have concluded that many students cannot use higher-order thinking processes.

In addition, standardized tests, which drive many state curricula, now test higher-order and critical thinking more rigorously. Yet standardized test scores continue to reveal an inability among large populations of students to think critically.

In 1991, the U. S. Department of Labor Secretary's Commission on Achieving Necessary Skills (SCANS) released its study on the state of education. In *What Work Requires of Schools*, SCANS stressed the need to emphasize critical thinking in all school curricula. In its publication, SCANS painted a bleak picture of the future. It questioned whether American businesses could maintain a high status in the world economy if students entering the work force could not think critically, solve problems, make decisions, or reason logically.

Businesses are also criticizing schools for not preparing students to meet the demands of the workplace, to face the challenges of the twenty-first century, to master the demands of a technologically advanced society, and to partake of the knowledge and opportunity for learning that technology provides.

Moreover, world issues increasingly impact social and political issues in the United States, and citizens need to be able to interpret and evaluate new information quickly.

The personal lives of teenagers have also become more complex. Teens today face more serious social, job, and health-related decisions than did teens of previous decades. Products designed specifically for the teenage market are more available now, and teens are inundated by pressures from advertisers vying for their attention and money.

As a result of these demands, language arts teachers are being called upon to place more emphasis on critical thinking and to develop appropriate activities that promote creative and critical thinking.

Teaching critical thinking is essential in language arts classes because of the close relationship between language and thinking. Language is a way of learning and thinking both in terms of one's ability to interpret and judge the validity of language and one's ability to use language to articulate ideas logically.

Teaching the higher-order thinking skills has become an imperative of the educational system. *Thinking It Through*, with its rich topics, formats, and activities, can serve the needs of both teachers and students.

Level	Title	Reading Level	Unit Topics
Book 1	Challenges	4/5	self-esteem, handling stress and pressure, peer pressure, nutrition, advertising, community volunteer work
Book 2	Community	6/7	citizenship, politics, freedoms of expression, advertising, consumerism, community volunteer work
Book 3	Changes	7/8	finding and getting a job, living independently, loaded and misleading language, consumerism, community volunteer work

THINKING IT THROUGH

Scope of Critical Thinking Skills

	KNOWING					COMPREHENDING			APPLYING							ANALYZING		
	Identifying	Observing	Recognizing	Distinguishing	Reading critically	Mapping	Applying	Brainstorming	Compiling	Examining	Gathering information	Generating	Summarizing	Supporting	Analyzing	Categorizing	Comparing and contrasting	Ordering
Book 1 Challenges																		
Unit 1	x		x					x		x	x	x	x		x	x		
Unit 2	x					x				x		x			x	x		
Unit 3	x										x				x			
Unit 4	x			x						x	x	x	x		x	x		
Unit 5	x										x				x		x	
Unit 6	x	x	x					x			x	x	x					
Book 2 Community																		
Unit 1	x		x							x	x	x	x	x	x			
Unit 2	x									x	x		x		x		x	
Unit 3	x							x					x				x	
Unit 4	x		x				x			x			x		x	x	x	
Unit 5	x			x				x							x	x		
Unit 6	x	x						x			x	x	x		x			
Book 3 Changes																		
Unit 1	x		x												x	x		
Unit 2	x			x						x		x	x		x	x		
Unit 3	x				x						x	x			x	x		
Unit 4	x			x	x												x	
Unit 5	x		x	x											x			
Unit 6	x																	

Skill groups: **SYNTHESIZING** spans *Interpreting* through *Debating*; **EVALUATING** spans *Drawing conclusions* through *Prioritizing*.

	Organizing	Questioning	Formulating	Interpreting	Planning	Predicting	Researching	Proposing	Synthesizing	Assessing	Debating	Drawing conclusions	Evaluating	Making decisions	Making inferences	Making judgments	Negotiating	Prioritizing
Book 1 Challenges																		
Unit 1			x					x		x		x	x	x	x			x
Unit 2				x	x							x	x			x	x	
Unit 3					x				x			x			x			
Unit 4	x	x		x				x				x	x		x			
Unit 5	x				x							x	x	x				
Unit 6					x	x	x		x			x	x					
Book 2 Community																		
Unit 1			x			x		x	x		x	x						
Unit 2						x		x	x	x	x	x	x		x			x
Unit 3	x		x	x	x							x			x			
Unit 4	x				x	x						x	x	x				
Unit 5					x		x					x	x	x		x		
Unit 6	x					x		x				x						
Book 3 Changes																		
Unit 1		x	x			x			x			x						x
Unit 2			x									x	x					
Unit 3				x								x						x
Unit 4				x								x	x		x			
Unit 5							x					x						
Unit 6	x	x				x			x			x	x					x

UNIT 1

Thinking About Your Future

BEGINNING THE UNIT

Unit Introduction (page 5)

Engaging the Students

When students have finished reading the unit introduction on page 5, help them create question wheels to start thinking critically about jobs. Have students work in pairs to make the wheels.

To model a question wheel on the chalkboard, draw a circle within a circle. Draw six spokes between the inner circle (the hub) and the outer circle to create six sections. Have students copy your model on paper.

Tell students to write *jobs* in the hub of the wheel and the question words *who, why, when, where, what,* and *how* between the spokes. Then have them generate one or more questions about jobs and write them in each spoke.

Students may generate questions like the following:

- **Who** are employers looking for?
- **Why** will being able to think critically help me get a good job?
- **When** should I begin job hunting?
- **Where** can I find a job?

- **What** kind of job do I want?
- **How** should I look for a job?

Allow students time to discuss the questions and possible answers. Explain that this strategy will help them answer questions as they work through the unit. Have students return to their wheels as they complete each lesson and the unit project. Ask if their answers changed after reading the lessons.

Thinking Strategy

Point out that critical thinkers ask questions about all aspects of a problem or topic. Explain that students can explore a topic better by using the "W" and "H" question words: *who, what, when, where, why,* and *how.*

What Works

Teachers have found that using a question wheel can help students generate and organize questions. Combining the "W" and "H" question strategy with the wheel may encourage students to broaden the ways in which they think and ask questions about an issue.

There's Life after a Job Interview (pages 6–8)

Before students read the story, initiate a class discussion in which students describe their expectations and fears about job hunting. If any students have had a job interview, invite them to relate their experiences.

Ask students to jot down thoughts and questions that they may have as they read the story. They may write their notes in their workbooks, or they may record them in their Think Pads. Have students save their questions for later discussions or future research.

Discussion Questions

Tell students that they may refer to their own experiences, as well as to the story, as they answer the following discussion questions. Point out that there are no right or wrong answers to these questions. You may wish to have students discuss the questions in pairs or in small groups before joining a class discussion.

1. Several points about job interviews were made in this story. Which point most surprised you? (Students may wish to scan the story before answering. Possible answers include the importance of dress, the fact that most people have had bad interviews, and the need to think about the kinds of questions that an interviewer is likely to ask.)

2. What mistakes do you think Shauna made in her interview? (Students might mention mistakes that are directly stated in the story, such as not understanding the job description. Students may also mention details that imply mistakes, such as Shauna's habits of playing with her hair and cracking jokes when she is nervous.)

3. If you were Shauna, what would you do differently when you apply for a job? (Have students brainstorm ideas, which may include Lucy's advice, corrections of mistakes that Shauna made, and ideas from students' personal experiences.)

ESL/LEP Strategy

Have ESL/LEP students talk about interview etiquette and job-hunting practices in their native countries. Encourage the rest of the class to ask questions that compare and contrast job-search practices in countries other than the United States.

Thinking Strategy

Explain to students that critical thinkers critique their interviews; that is, they think about what they handled well and what they could have done differently or better. They look at both their strengths and weaknesses. In this way, critical thinkers are able to learn from their mistakes.

TEACHING THE LESSONS

Lesson 1: Identifying Goals, Interests, and Skills (pages 9–11)

Thinking Skill Objectives:

- Students will **identify** their job goals, interests, and skills.
- Students will **analyze** jobs to decide which might be right for them.

- Students will **prioritize** their goals, interests, and skills.
- Students will read and **evaluate** "Help Wanted" advertisements.
- Students will **identify** sources for finding jobs.

Content Objective:

- Students will determine which jobs are most suited to their personal goals, interests, and skills.

Have students read the lesson introduction on page 9. Then explain that this lesson has two purposes:

- to help them think critically about which job might be right for them
- to help them identify the job they want in "Help Wanted" advertisements

Using the Graphic Organizer (page 9)

Model one or two responses for the goal-centered cluster map. You may also want to model the interest-centered and skills-centered cluster maps on the chalkboard. Have students continue filling in the maps individually.

Get students started making charts by modeling how to transfer ideas from the cluster maps to the appropriate chart columns.

Sidenote Connection

You might want to make students aware of the sidenote "Skills Employers Seek." This information might affect the way in which students complete their cluster maps and the job duties they list in the unit project.

Cooperative Learning

After students have filled in the columns on their charts, you may wish to have them share their responses using the following cooperative learning activity.

Ask the entire class to stand up. Invite one volunteer to identify his or her top item in the "Goals" column. Tell students with the same or a similar response to sit down. Ask another student to name a first item for the "Interests" column and have all students with a similar priority sit down. Call on a third volunteer to name a priority for "Skills," and have students who share that answer sit down. Repeat this process for first items under "Goals," and so on, until all students are seated.

This activity gives students a chance to compare what they consider to be top priorities without taking the time to have each student speak.

What Works

Teachers have found that cooperative learning strategies give students a chance to compare and learn from each other's thinking processes.

ESL/LEP Strategy

Ask your ESL/LEP students to bring to class examples of "Help Wanted" advertisements from newspapers and magazines written in their first language. Encourage them to describe the ways in which the advertisements are like and unlike job advertisements in this country.

Responses (page 11)

Answers will vary.

1. Students should choose jobs that reflect their highest priority goals, interests, and skills.

2. In students' explanations for their choices, they should state the ways in which the job reflects their high-priority interests.

3. Students should state the ways in which the job will use the skills they named in their charts.

4. Some students may mention jobs that say "will train" or "no experience necessary." Others may state positions that are similar to part-time jobs they have already held.

5. Some students may name jobs that say "career," "advancement possible," or that offer benefits. Others will list jobs that will enhance or further their goals, skills, and interests.

Thinking Journal

You might have students write in their Thinking Journals the answer to the second question in the "Evaluation" box on page 11.

Ask students to describe how making lists helps them to think critically. Also encourage them to explain the process they used to identify their goals, skills, and interests for this lesson.

Evaluation Tip

Consider evaluating and grading students on their answers to the questions on page 11. You might want to assign two points for each answer, with a total of ten points. Points may also be given for students' willingness to participate in discussions and activities in this lesson and in the quality of their participation.

What Works

Teachers find that students focus better on their work when they have been told how the work will be evaluated. If you are using a letter or number scale, explain the criteria for each letter or number.

Lesson 2: Predicting Interview Questions (pages 12–13)

Thinking Skill Objectives:

- Students will **predict** questions that an employer might ask.
- Students will **analyze** a position to decide what kind of worker should be hired.
- Students will **identify** the qualities that an employee should have for a specific position.

Content Objective:

- Students will learn about the job interview process.

Have students read the lesson introduction on page 12. Then explain that Lesson 2 will prepare them for job interviews by helping them to predict the kinds of questions they may be asked.

Have students write the name of a company in the space provided. Suggest that they design a logo or a creative way of writing the company's name, if they wish.

Point out that they should know or research information about the kind of work involved in the job they describe. Then tell students to fill out the chart on page 12 individually.

Cooperative Learning Strategy

Instead of having students complete the chart individually, you might wish to give them an opportunity to share their responses with the class, using the following cooperative learning strategy.

First, have students form small groups to decide on a name for their company and the position they are offering. Company and position titles may be chosen from the ones that members had previously invented. Then allow students to discuss which qualities they want in their ideal employee. Ideas may come from the charts they had filled in individually. Finally, have them make a poster-size chart of "Qualities of the Best Candidate for the Job." Have each group then share its work with the class.

Thinking Journal

Have students record in their Thinking Journals the process they used to predict interview questions. Also encourage them to write whether their predictions helped them to perform better in the mock interview. Tell students that if they did not predict questions well, they should describe how they might predict questions better in the future.

Thinking Strategy

Tell students that critical thinkers try to understand situations better by "putting themselves in someone else's shoes." Looking at a situation such as a job interview from the other person's point of view is an excellent way to prepare for it.

What Works

Teachers have found that asking students to "try on" a different point of view can help them generate new ideas, anticipate problems, and reflect on their thinking processes.

Responses (page 13)

Answers will vary according to which four interview questions a student chooses. The following is a possible list. (Explain to students that the answers they write should refer to the position they named on page 12.)

1. Students may mention language and computer courses, auto mechanics, or other courses that would prepare them for the position.
2. Some students may name specific skills; others may name qualities such as "an eagerness to learn" or "honesty."
3. The clever answer is "I work too hard."
4. Students may use the qualities they listed in the chart on page 12.

ESL/LEP Strategy

Role-playing is an excellent way for students with limited English to generate interview questions. Rather than have ESL/LEP students write lists of questions, allow them to make notes in English or in their native language. Students should use their notes as they work in pairs to role-play interviewer and job candidate.

Discussion (page 13)

Focus attention on the critical thinking needed to solve these "sticky" situations. You may wish to begin the discussion with a response of your own. Ask students if they think the solution you offered would work. Have them tell why it would or wouldn't work.

Continue the discussion in this way. Encourage students to give positive feedback to responses but allow them to politely state why a solution might not work.

Alternative to the Discussion

Instead of having a whole-class discussion, you may wish to have students analyze the questions in small groups. Place at least one person with strong communication skills in each group.

Have group members appoint a secretary to record their responses. Then allow groups to discuss the "sticky" situations for ten minutes.

When the time is up, have each secretary take a turn reading and explaining members' responses. Encourage groups to compare and defend their solutions.

Thinking Strategy

Explain to students that critical thinkers listen attentively during discussions. As they listen, they let their minds build on the ideas of others. By keeping their minds open, critical listeners often develop creative and original ideas.

What Works

Teachers have found that assigning the roles of listener and speaker to students and then changing those roles encourages students to develop critical listening skills.

Sidenote Connection

Have students read the definition of *predicting* in the sidenote. Encourage volunteers to share examples of times when they have used what they already know to tell what might happen in the future.

Evaluation Tip

Consider allowing students to evaluate their own work in this lesson. First, have students read the questions in the "Evaluation" box. Then have them develop and record their own rating system. Students may develop a letter code or a number scale. Whichever they choose, have them write descriptors for each letter or number. For example, "S" might represent a satisfactory score or 3 might represent an excellent score on a scale of 1–3.

What Works

Teachers find that students often concentrate better and work with more interest when they can develop their own rating scales. When students practice self-evaluation on short assignments, they are better able to transfer this skill to more complex assignments.

Lesson 3: Asking Questions on the Job (pages 14–15)

Thinking Skill Objectives:

- Students will **ask questions** that a new employee might have about a job.
- Students will **categorize** information to anticipate what they might find in an employee handbook.
- Students will **identify** difficulties they might have on a job.

Content Objective:

- Students will learn about job responsibilities and rules.

Explain to students that in this lesson they will imagine that they are new employees. They will learn the kinds of questions to ask to get the information needed to do their jobs well.

Have students begin the lesson by reading the introduction on page 14.

Using the Graphic Organizer (page 14)

Have students fill in the graphic organizer individually, using a colored marker. Then ask them to share their information with a classmate. Have students use another color to add new information from their partner's responses to their own graphic organizer.

ESL/LEP Strategy

Students from other countries may not be familiar with details of working environments in this country. Suggest that they look through magazines and newspapers for pictures of people at work. This strategy can help students to imagine themselves working on a job.

When ESL/LEP students do the graphic organizer in this lesson, pair them with a student who has strong verbal and writing skills.

Cooperative Learning Strategy

As an alternative to having students read the employee handbook and complete the chart individually, you may wish to involve them in the following cooperative learning strategy.

Divide the class into three groups and give each group a different colored marker. Write the directions for each pair of questions from the chart on a separate sheet of paper and hand one page to each group. Have a volunteer from each group act as the recorder.

Give each group five minutes to discuss and write two questions. Then signal them to stop writing.

Collect and redistribute the papers so that each group has directions for a new pair of questions. Have the recorders again write their group's questions with the colored marker assigned to the group. Continue in this way until each group has written a pair of questions on each sheet.

As a class, have students read and compare the questions that the groups wrote. You may wish to have students answer the questions in a class discussion or assign the questions to individuals or small groups.

Sidenote Connection

You may wish to have students read and report on one or more of the books listed in "Bookshelf." Other titles that you might recommend include the following:

Careers in the Computer Industry,
  by Laura Green.
Tell Me About Yourself: How to Interview Anyone From Your Friends to Famous People,
  by D. L. Maybery.
Early Stages: The Professional Theater and the Young Actor, by Walter Williamson.
Working Kids on Working, by Sheila Cole.
How to Use Your Community as a Resource,
  by Helen Carey.

What Works

Teachers have found that encouraging reading stimulates students' interest in new ideas and helps them to become more flexible in their thinking. Teachers also find that students' ability to be critical readers improves when they are given an active role in choosing, discussing, and recommending reading materials.

Thinking Strategy

Explain to students that critical thinkers are also critical readers. A critical reader actively looks for key ideas, reasons, supporting examples, and other features in books, magazine articles, newspapers, and other texts. The critical reader engages in a mental dialogue with the writer.

Evaluation Tip

You may wish to evaluate and grade students' reports on the books suggested in "Bookshelf" or on other books you might recommend.

Give students the following five guidelines before they write their reports:

1. The book report should briefly tell what the book is about.
2. The report should give the student's opinion of the book.
3. The title and author of the book should be stated at the beginning of the report.
4. Students should explain why they would or would not recommend the book to other students.
5. Students should tell what they learned from the book about job hunting, interviewing, or careers.

Consider assigning two points in a grading scale to each of the five guidelines for reports. Inform students of the scale you plan to use.

ESL/LEP Strategy

Students whose first language is not English may feel more comfortable reading books in their native language. If they do choose to read a book that is written in another language, however, encourage them to write the report in English so that it may be shared with the class or graded.

MAKING CONNECTIONS

The Job Interview: A Two-Way Exchange (pages 16–19)

Thinking Skill Objectives:

- Students will **identify** the best jobs for them.
- Students will **formulate** a summary of the job that they want.
- Students will **predict** questions that an interviewer might ask.

Content Objectives:

- Students will write interview questions.
- Students will role-play an interview, with partners taking turns being the interviewer and the applicant.

Before beginning the unit project, you may wish to have students briefly review what they did and learned in Lessons 1, 2, and 3. Point out that they may use graphic organizers, charts, or information from the unit lessons as tools while working on the unit project. Then have students read the project introduction on page 16.

Step 1: Identifying the Target Job (page 16)

Before students begin brainstorming kinds of jobs, you may wish to have them think about elements of a job that they would especially like. On the chalkboard, write the following idea starter:

I would especially like to work _____.

Encourage students to think of several ways to complete the sentence. Write their responses on the chalkboard under the idea starter. Responses may include the following:

in a quiet place	with words
with computers	with people
alone	indoors
outdoors	in a city
with paint	with animals
on cars	with children
in a garden	where I can travel

What Works

Many teachers have found that completing idea starters, or open-ended statements, helps students identify their options.

Thinking Strategy

Explain to students that when critical thinkers make choices, they first identify their preferences. By identifying what they like, they will have criteria for judging their options.

Step 2: Writing a Job Summary (page 17)

Partners may either write their summaries individually and then compare what they have written, or they may write a summary jointly.

ESL/LEP Strategy

Suggest that ESL/LEP students look again at "Help Wanted" advertisements for examples of duties that are expected with particular jobs. Point out that job titles that sound similar to titles used in their native languages may in fact have quite different meanings and duties. Remind them to read the job descriptions carefully and to use a bilingual dictionary if necessary.

Step 3: Predicting Questions (page 17)

Suggest that students look again at the interview questions they wrote in Lesson 2. Remind them that thinking about the needs of the employer, as played by their partner, will help them predict the questions that will be asked.

To help students predict the five most likely questions that they will be asked, you may wish to draw an inverted triangle on the chalkboard. At the top (wide end of the triangle) write: "What the employer most wants to know."

At the bottom (point of the triangle) write: "What the employer is least interested in knowing."

Draw and number five write-on lines in the triangle. Tell students to copy the triangle and write at the top the question they are most likely to be asked. The second most likely question should be written next in the triangle, and so on.

Step 4: Writing Questions to Ask a Job Applicant (page 18)

If students have trouble switching their perspective to the interviewer's point of view, suggest that they write their questions in a thought balloon. You may want to model a stick-figure person with a thought

What Works

Many teachers have found that making thought balloons often helps students understand another person's point of view.

balloon on the chalkboard, or bring in cartoons or comic strips in which thought balloons are used.

Step 5: Interviewing (pages 18–19)

Give partners ample opportunity to practice their interviews before they act them out in front of the class. Students may enjoy using some simple props, such as briefcases and clipboards. They may also enjoy having the "interviewer" sit at your desk.

Cooperative Learning Strategy

Before pairs present their interviews to the class, match them with a second pair of students. Have the two sets of partners take turns presenting their interviews and acting as the audience.

When acting as the audience, students should listen critically, taking notes and preparing feedback. Instruct audience pairs to give five responses, at least two of which should be positive. Remind them to be polite and encouraging and to accompany criticisms with carefully worded suggestions for improvement.

Remind students that they should use only those suggestions that they think will improve their interviews.

Thinking Journal

Ask students to write in their Thinking Journals an evaluation of their performance on Step 3 of the project. Encourage them to compare and contrast their performance at this stage with their performance on Lesson 2. Ask students: Did your ability to predict questions improve? Why or why not? Was the process you used to predict questions for the project the same as the one you used for the lesson? If not, what did you change? If so, was it a successful process the second time? Why or why not?

Step 6: Evaluating Your Project (page 19)

You may want to have students pool their ideas on which criteria to use in evaluating the projects. On the chalkboard, write suggestions students want to share. Then allow pairs to adapt these ideas as they develop their own criteria.

Students may enjoy voting for the pair they felt conducted the best interview. Before the vote, however, have students agree on some criteria for scoring. As an alternative to having just one winning pair, consider using categories such as "Best Questions" and "Best Answers."

Thinking Strategy

Explain to students that critical thinkers value suggestions from others. Tell student pairs that as they help each other evaluate their work, they should accompany any critical responses with ideas for improving performance. Remind them, too, that they should use only those suggestions that they think are appropriate.

What Works

Many teachers find that students often evaluate their work more thoughtfully and honestly when they work on the evaluation with a peer.

Unit Test (page 20)

In addition to, or as an alternative to, the unit project, you may wish to have students complete the unit test.

Responses

1. c. The employer is interested in finding the best possible person for the job.

2. Answers will vary. Students may mention that thinking critically about their own skills and accomplishments will help them find a job that they like and for which they are suited.

3. Answers will vary. Students may suggest stressing their strengths and moving away from the subject while remaining honest with the interviewer.

4. Answers will vary. Essays should include thinking about what kind of job to apply for, searching for the job, reading "Help Wanted" Advertisements, preparing for an interview, and predicting interview questions.

Getting the Job You Want

BEGINNING THE UNIT

Unit Introduction (page 21)

Engaging the Students

Have students read the unit introduction on page 21. Then divide the class into pairs or small groups. Ask each group to bring to class the "Help Wanted" section from various newspapers, especially from Sunday newspapers.

Ask groups to use colored pencils to circle paperwork requested in the job advertisements. Students may circle phrases such as the following:

- send/FAX résumé to
- send salary requirements
- résumé + cover letter
- job/salary history

Have students clip out representative advertisements and display them on a class poster. Make sure students understand the meaning of phrases and abbreviations in the advertisements. Then begin a class discussion about job hunting. Use the following questions as discussion starters.

1. Why do employers want applicants to send résumés if the applicants will be filling out an application form?

2. Why do employers want a cover letter with résumés?

3. If employers have already decided how much they are going to pay, why do they want to know salary histories and requirements?

4. Why is it important to think critically when reading job advertisements and writing cover letters and résumés?

Then ask students what questions they have about job hunting.

Explain to students that precise answers to these questions need not be given now and that the answers will become clearer to them as they complete the lessons in Unit 2. You may want to have students briefly discuss the questions now and assign them to individuals or groups to answer at the end of the unit.

Thinking Strategy

Explain to students that critical thinkers ask questions to learn the reasoning behind procedures. By knowing or predicting the answers to their questions, critical thinkers have a better understanding of how best to proceed.

What Works

Many teachers have found that students are more responsive to a subject when they have had a chance to think about why they are studying it or when they have determined a purpose for their study.

How to Land the Perfect Job (pages 22–23)

Before beginning "How to Land the Perfect Job," help students determine a purpose for reading the story. Suggest that as they read they ask themselves the question: Is Charlie's experience in job hunting similar to or different from my experience(s)? Students who have not started job hunting might ask themselves: How will Charlie's experience help me to look for a job?

ESL/LEP Strategy

One of the elements of English that many ESL/LEP students find difficult is the extensive use of idioms. Following is a list of idioms in "How to Land the Perfect Job." Before ESL/LEP students begin reading the story, you may want to go over the idioms with them, or you may assign the list to them to research. Mention that there are several good American English-idiom dictionaries available in libraries and bookstores. Also consider having students with strong verbal skills work on the idioms with individuals or small groups of ESL/LEP students.

The following are idioms found in "How to Land the Perfect Job."

- land a job
- give it to you straight
- come home winners
- whole town turns out
- last of the big-time . . .
- check out
- hit the newspapers
- there's a catch
- toss in a couple of jokes
- once I get into it . . .
- I'm really flying
- he's been after me about . . .
- I go for the gold
- I climb the highest mountain
- play it straight

Discussion Questions

Explain to students that there are no right or wrong answers to the following discussion questions. They may use the story as a springboard for ideas, but answers should also refer to their own experiences. You may wish to have students discuss the story with partners or in small groups to answer the questions.

1. Why is landing one's first job a memorable event for most people? (Students may suggest that a first job represents one's entrance into the adult world, that it marks the beginning of a new episode in one's life, or that it puts one on the path toward independence.)

2. Charlie tells us several things about job hunting in this story. What do you think was the most important point that he made? (Students may mention the importance of being honest, the need to read job advertisements carefully, or the importance of creating a good first impression with a well-written letter and résumé.)

3. Was Frank wise to hire Charlie? Do you think Charlie would make a good employee? (Students who think Charlie would make a good employee might mention his determination and readiness to learn from his mistakes. They may also mention that he is willing to work and that he seems to take his new job seriously. Charlie's detractors might mention that he looks for the easy way first and only does things "the right way" after his first approach has failed.)

4. Give an example of how Charlie used critical thinking skills. (Possible answers are that Charlie used critical thinking skills when he read the ads critically, chose one job for which he was qualified, revised the letter, decided to use the typewriter, chose to leave nonessential information out of his résumé (e.g., the hot-dog job), predicted that untrue information would be easily identified on the application.)

TEACHING THE LESSONS

Lesson 1: Categorizing Job Skills and Preferences (pages 24–25)

Thinking Skill Objectives:

- Students will **identify** their skills and interests.
- Students will **categorize** job skills and job preferences.
- Students will **draw conclusions** about their skills and interests.

Content Objective:

- Students will learn about categories of jobs and the skills those jobs require.

Have students read the introduction to Lesson 1 on page 24. Tell students that this lesson will ask them to think critically about the interests and skills they will bring to the job market.

Cooperative Learning

Use the following cooperative learning activity to help students understand that not all people share the same interests and abilities.

After students have circled items that interest them on the chart on page 24, ask them to compare their choices with those of a partner. Then have two pairs of students join together to compare their four sets of responses. Have them include the following two questions in their discussions:

1. Of the items you circled, which would you name as your first, second, and third choices or preferences? Explain your response.

2. What would happen if people entering the job market all had the same interests and skills? Describe such a situation.

You may wish to have students remain in their groups of four to brainstorm responses to the question, "What else do you like to do that isn't listed?" Have representatives read the responses from each group. List their answers on the chalkboard. Select several items from the list to discuss with students how the interests would transfer to job skills.

Using the Graphic Organizer (page 25)

You may wish to walk around the classroom as students are filling in the chart to see if anyone needs individual help categorizing the list of skills.

Remind students that they may include in the chart the responses they wrote to the question, "What else do you like to do that isn't listed?"

When students have completed their graphic organizers, ask them to answer the two questions that follow it. You may wish to allow students to discuss the questions as a class before they write their responses. Possible answers include the following:

1. In a discussion, students may mention that most of the skills they circled in the first chart proved to be related—that is, most were categorized together in one or two columns in the graphic organizer. Students should conclude that their interests tend to fall into one or two of the categories listed. A written response may be, "I like working with ideas best. I also like working with things."

2. Students' written responses should state the importance of finding jobs that they enjoy and for which they are suited. In discussion, students may explain that they would have a better chance of succeeding at a job and of holding the job longer if it appealed to their skills and interests.

Sidenote Connection

Students might find the sidenote "Categories of Jobs" on page 24 to be a helpful resource as they answer the two questions that follow the graphic organizer.

As students work on the graphic organizer, you may wish to make them aware of the definition of *categorize* in the sidenote on page 25.

Thinking Strategy

Explain to students that critical thinkers often categorize items so that they can see their choices more clearly. One critical thinker who used this list-making strategy before drawing conclusions was Benjamin Franklin.

Thinking Journal

Have students write in their Thinking Journals the process they used to categorize their skills, interests, and talents. Also ask them to write instances in their daily lives when they need to categorize things.

What Works

Teachers have found that students are better able to draw conclusions when they first categorize facts or information. Being able to compare the data with other sources also helps students to evaluate their choices.

Discussion (page 25)

Guide students through the discussion, allowing differences in opinion. Some students may feel that employers are very likely to verify information on résumés; other students may disagree. Some students may state that the size of the company or the kind of job would affect the likelihood of an applicant being checked out. Ask if the risk would be worth taking. You may need to point out that falsifying information on applications for union, civil-service, and bonded jobs can be more serious than with other jobs.

You may wish to suggest a specific job for the friend in the first question in order to make the situation come alive for students. Choose a line of work that was often cited by students in their graphic organizers or in discussions. Emphasize the importance of using critical thinking to solve problems like the one portrayed in this activity.

Alternative to the Discussion

As an alternative to the discussion question on page 25, you may wish to have students generate and discuss their own questions.

Divide the class into groups of three or four. Give each group several 3" x 5" cards and tell them to write one question about job hunting on the front of each card. Have them also write their answers to the questions on the back of each card.

Explain to students that they should write questions that can have more than one answer. Tell them to avoid questions that have definite right or wrong answers or questions that can be answered "yes" or "no." Encourage them to write questions that will stimulate discussion and that will require students to use critical thinking skills to answer.

Collect and shuffle the cards. Ask volunteers to read the cards aloud one at a time for class discussion. After each question has been answered, have the volunteer read the back of the card. Ask how the group's answer varied from the class's answer.

What Works

Many teachers have found that students are motivated to think critically when they are given the opportunity to present, defend, and argue against a variety of opinions or points of view. Discussions that encourage opposing points of view encourage students to apply the thinking skills they have learned.

ESL/LEP Strategy

Students whose first language is not English or who have limited language skills often find it difficult to follow class discussions. The more absorbed and aggressive that participants become in a lively discussion, the more quickly they speak and the more their use of idiomatic language increases.

To help ESL/LEP students get the most out of a class discussion without quelling the enthusiasm of participants, record the discussion on a cassette tape. ESL/LEP students can listen to the tape later to make sure they understood all the points that were being made. Encourage them to stop the tape and jot down idioms, figures of speech, and words that are unfamiliar. You may wish to explain to ESL/LEP students excerpted ideas that they found to be confusing, or you may ask other students to explain difficult segments. Unfamiliar vocabulary and phrases can be assigned to ESL/LEP students as homework.

Allow them to replay the tape as often as they wish. Encourage them to stop the tape when a question has been posed and to state their own responses aloud. If a second tape player is available, have them record the discussion and their responses on a second tape so that nothing is erased on the original.

As ESL/LEP students become more confident with their language skills, encourage them to participate as much as possible in class discussions.

Evaluation Tip

You may wish to evaluate and grade students on their responses to the questions following the graphic organizer. Consider evaluating how well they applied information from the charts to draw appropriate conclusions. You might use a grading scale of 1–5 for each question. Add the scores together to assign a grade that could be applied to a scale of 1–10.

Lesson 2: Analyzing and Assessing Job Skills (pages 26–27)

Thinking Skill Objectives:

- Students will **examine** their work experience and extra-curricular activities.
- Students will **identify** the skills they have gained from their experience.
- Students will **analyze** their skills.
- Students will **assess** the skills to determine which will transfer to the jobs they desire.

Content Objective:

- Students will learn how to transfer their skills to job situations.

Ask students to read the lesson introduction on page 26. Explain that in this lesson they will learn how to think critically about the skills they have and about how those skills can be made marketable.

Have volunteers tell what they wrote for their job objectives. Write several responses on the chalkboard. Initiate a brief discussion of the kinds of skills that might be needed for each of the positions named in the job objectives.

Sidenote Connection

After students have read the sidenote "Skills That Transfer to a Job," divide students into groups of three or four. Tell the groups to brainstorm the skill-making experiences they have had. Have one member of each group act as recorder, writing the responses on a posterboard or chalkboard. Display the lists where they can be seen by all students.

Using the Graphic Organizer (page 27)

Tell students that as they complete their graphic organizers they may refer to Kima's experiences and skills and to students' responses generated during brainstorming sessions.

Explain that before they circle skills on the chart, they should think about the job objective that each wrote. Tell students to focus on the skills needed for the kind of job that each has selected.

ESL/LEP Strategy

Students from other countries may have had job-hunting experiences that are very different from those of the rest of the class. Invite them to tell the class about their experiences and encourage questions from students.

You may wish to incorporate into this question/answer activity some questions of your own that will help ESL/LEP students analyze skills they have learned from their experiences.

Cooperative Learning Strategy

After students have written the paragraph telling why they are a strong candidate for the job they want, divide them into pairs. Explain to students that they will exchange papers and that each person will act as his or her partner's editor.

Tell students that before they give their paragraph to a partner, they should check it carefully. Advise students to ask themselves the following questions as they reread their work.

- Is there a topic sentence that expresses the main idea, or the skills I have to do the job?
- Do the other sentences support the main idea by naming a valuable skill that I have?
- Have I made any errors in spelling, punctuation, capitalization, or grammar?

Explain to students that when they are editing a writer's work, they should try to make positive, constructive comments about specific parts of the paragraph. Tell editors to ask themselves the following questions as they read their partner's paragraph.

- Would the paragraph convince an employer to interview the writer for a job? Why or why not?
- Are their any errors in spelling, mechanics, or grammar that would give a bad impression?

Allow pairs to discuss each other's paragraphs. Tell students to listen carefully to their editor's suggestions. Remind editors to be positive and respectful in their criticisms.

Give students time to revise their paragraphs. Advise them to use only those suggestions that seem to improve their work.

Invite volunteers to read their paragraphs to the class.

What Works

Many teachers have found that peer editing allows students to learn from what the writer does right, as well as from the writer's mistakes. Teachers have also found that students are more likely to revise their writing when it has been edited by a peer.

Thinking Strategy

Explain to students that when critical thinkers write they keep in mind an audience and a purpose for writing. In this activity, the audience is a prospective employer and the purpose for writing is to convince the employer to interview the writer for a job.

Thinking Journal

Have students describe in their Thinking Journals the process they used to determine the skills they will bring to a job. Encourage volunteers to share their entries with the class.

Sidenote Connection

Ask students to read the "Bookshelf" sidenote. Then have them find in the library or from another source one book about making career decisions or applying for a job. The book may be one from the "Bookshelf" list, or it may be another book of their choice.

Have students bring the books to class and display them in the classroom. You might consider giving extra credit to students who read and report on a book.

Discussion (page 27)

Encourage one or two volunteers to restate the main idea of the discussion in their own words. Then have students individually brainstorm responses to the question, "What might happen if you don't look to the future when you think about getting a job?"

After five minutes, begin the class discussion by inviting students to share their responses and opinions about the question. Encourage students to use details and examples to support their points.

What Works

Many teachers have found that when students restate ideas in their own words, they often clarify for themselves what might have been confusing.

Alternative to the Discussion

As an alternative to the discussion, you may wish to use the following activity.

Divide students into groups of three or four. Tell students that each group represents a company that is planning to hire new employees. Have students role-play the parts of employers, deciding which job experience and skills they will be looking for in their candidates.

To begin, groups should decide what kind of job opening their company will have. They may then copy the graphic organizer in this lesson onto posterboard. Tell them to change the chart heads to "Candidate's Experience" and "Skills We Need."

Give groups time to brainstorm, discuss, and develop a written profile of their desired candidate. Have them share their profiles with the class.

What Works

Teachers have found that role-playing offers students the opportunity to analyze a situation from another point of view.

Evaluation Tip

Consider evaluating and grading students on their revisions of the paragraphs they wrote in this lesson. You may wish to have students hand in both their first-draft paragraphs and their revisions so that you can check whether needed corrections were made and whether writers made any unnecessary or inappropriate changes suggested by editors.

Lesson 3: Interpreting Instructions on an Application Form (pages 28–29)

Thinking Skill Objectives:

- Students will **read critically** the various parts of an application form.
- Students will **interpret** directions for filling in a job application.

Content Objective:

- Students will practice completing a job application form.

Have students read the introduction to this lesson on page 28. Explain that this lesson has two purposes:

- to help students become critical readers of job application forms so that they can avoid misinterpreting the instructions
- to give students advice and practice in completing applications

Give students time to read the chart. Then ask them the following questions. Answers will vary. Possible answers are provided in parentheses.

1. Why do you think blue or black ink is preferred? (Dark ink shows up better when photocopied. Pencil allows the possibility of someone altering an applicant's form.)

2. Why do they want you to write the position for which you are applying? (There may be more than one position for which applications are being taken at the company.)

3. Why are applicants requested to write last names first? (Applications may be filed alphabetically according to last names.)

4. Why would it matter whether the applicant checks or circles items? (The employer is looking for someone who can follow directions.)

5. The form says "Do not write below this line." Why not fill in the information below the line if you know the answers? (Parts of the form may need to be filled out by office personnel.)

6. Why bother writing a current address if it is the same as the permanent address? (Never leave spaces blank. Employers may think you overlooked the question or don't want to give that information.)

7. Why fill in an employment history if you are supplying a résumé? (Employers want the same format on all job histories so that they can compare candidate's backgrounds easily.)

8. Why not just say, "I was fired," if it is the truth? (Without telling an untruth, this information can be phrased in a way that is more flattering to the applicant.)

Cooperative Learning Strategy

Before students complete the application form, help them organize their educational and work histories by modeling a timeline on the chalkboard. Allow students to work in pairs or small groups as they make personal timelines.

Thinking Strategy

Explain to students that critical thinkers often use graphic aids to help them conceptualize information.

What Works

Teachers have found that timelines are an effective way to help students organize chronological data, including personal information, such as the various schools students have attended or the jobs they have held. Timelines help students to connect dates with events and to put that information in time order.

 ## Thinking Journal

Have students evaluate their ability to interpret instructions in their Thinking Journals. As a class, develop the criteria by which students will evaluate themselves.

Evaluation Tip

You may wish to evaluate and grade students on their completion of the application form. Remind students to follow the guidelines in the "Hints for Application Forms" sidenote. Explain that students will *not* be graded according to who in the class would be best for a job, but on how well each student fills out the form.

MAKING CONNECTIONS

Applying for a Job (pages 30–33)

Thinking Skill Objectives:

- Students will **summarize** their educational background, skills, accomplishments, and work history.
- Students will write to **persuade** employers to read their résumés.
- Students will **develop** an application form.

Content Objectives:

- Students will write a résumé.
- Students will write a cover letter.
- Students will complete the application they have created.
- Students will publish their résumé, cover letter, and application form in a class book.

Have students read the introduction to "Making Connections" on page 30. Then invite volunteers to tell what they have learned in this unit about planning to apply for a job.

Step 1: Writing a Résumé (pages 30–31)

You may wish to briefly check students responses to "My Job Choice" and the list of four skills to make sure they are on the right track before they continue the unit project.

Although the simple résumé model shown is all most students will need, you may wish to mention that libraries have books containing other résumé layouts. Students who have access to a computer may be interested in the résumé templates now available on many word-processing programs.

Warn students against trying to cram too much information on a résumé. Suggest that they try to leave at least one fourth of the page as white space. Explain that nonessential details can be saved for possible use in the interview.

ESL/LEP Strategy

Remind students that they should include on their résumés the name of a country (other than the United States) after the name of any city in that country.

Suggest, too, that the English spellings of all place names be used on a résumé.

Step 2: Writing a Cover Letter (pages 31–32)

Guide students through the parts of the cover letter. Explain that it is important for students to follow the form of a standard business letter even though certain information, such as the sender's address, appears on an enclosed résumé.

Cooperative Learning Strategy

As an alternative to having students write letters individually, consider the following cooperative learning activity.

Divide students into groups of three. Ask each group to find in a telephone book the name and address of a company for which they would like to work. Have them name a possible position with that company. Then tell them to follow the model on page 32 to write letters of application for that position.

Have each group member write a different paragraph of the letter. The person writing the first paragraph should also be responsible for the heading, inside address, and greeting. The student who writes the third paragraph should add the closing and signature. Have the person who does the middle paragraph address the envelope.

Finished letters and envelopes may be displayed on a bulletin board.

Step 3: Creating an Application Form (pages 32–33)

Before beginning this step, you may wish to have students review what they learned in Lesson 3, "Interpreting Instructions on an Application Form."

Before dividing the class into groups, invite students who have applied for jobs to tell the class about any additional details that were on the forms they completed.

Thinking Strategy

Explain to students that critical thinkers bring to situations whatever information they think they will need. By preparing and bringing helpful tools, critical thinkers can feel more relaxed in the situation and will therefore be better able to focus on the task.

What Works

Many teachers have found that having students think about and prepare information to be transferred is a useful strategy not only for completing application forms but also for taking open-book tests. Teachers have found that students often prepare more thoroughly, and usually learn more in the process, when they are able to bring information into a testing situation.

Step 4: Publishing and Evaluating (page 33)

In addition to making a copy for the classroom, consider having students make a copy of their publication for each member of the class if resources for photocopying are available. Individual copies can be bound by stapling or sewing pages together, and a cardboard cover can be made for each book. Students can then add a table of contents and an index.

Moreover, a copy of *Help Wanted* would be a nice addition to the school library.

Unit Test (page 34)

In addition to, or as an alternative to, the unit project, you may wish to have students complete the unit test.

Responses

1. c. The cover letter should be a short introduction to the résumé enclosed.

2. d. The purpose of a résumé is to convince an employer to interview the applicant for a job.

3. Answers will vary. Students may suggest adding personal information that emphasizes accomplishments and skills or the candidate's ability to get along with others. Information about race, religion, or marital status should not be included.

4. Answers will vary. Students should mention most of the following criteria:
   - neatness
   - appropriateness of applicant's educational background and work history
   - suitability of applicant's skills for the job
   - statement of job objective
   - inclusion of applicant's address and telephone number
   - an interesting and well-written cover letter.

is not. Critical thinkers, therefore, often look for likenesses and differences between things. By comparing and contrasting two things or situations, it is possible to understand each better.

Living Independently

BEGINNING THE UNIT

Unit Introduction (page 35)

Engaging the Students

Ask students to read the unit introduction on page 35. Then have them make a Venn diagram to help them compare the similarities and differences between living at home and living independently.

Explain that to make a Venn diagram, students simply draw two circles that overlap. You may wish to model one on the chalkboard first.

Tell students that the middle section (the overlapping part) is where students should list things that are *alike* about living at home and living independently. An example might be "getting up in time for school or work."

In the left circle, students should list things about living at home that are *different* from living independently, such as not paying for meals. In the right circle, students should list things about living independently that are *different* from being dependent on others, such as paying for rent.

Tell students that as they think of more similarities and differences, they can add them to their Venn diagrams.

Thinking Strategy

Explain to students that sometimes we can better understand what something *is* by thinking about what it

What Works

Teachers have found that using a Venn diagram often helps students compare likenesses and differences more easily. Making a Venn diagram is simple, and it can be adapted to many situations and subject areas.

I Want To Be Me! (pages 36–37)

Ask students to read the magazine article, "I Want to Be Me!" Suggest that as students read the article they should write on their Think Pads questions or ideas they may want to discuss later.

Cooperative Learning Strategy

Instead of having students read "I Want to Be Me!" individually, consider doing the following cooperative learning activity.

Invite volunteers to read the magazine article aloud to the class. After each paragraph is read, have the student who read it answer questions about the section from the class. Tell students they may ask comprehension questions, such as, "How old was Aaron when he got his own apartment?" Students may also ask questions that require the reader to give an opinion, such as, "Do you think Aaron is too young to live on his own?"

You may wish to have readers answer three or four questions before moving on to the next volunteer and paragraph.

Creating Diary Entries

Divide students into small groups after they have finished reading the "I Want to Be Me!" article. Explain that each group will write a diary entry for one of the following characters:

- Aaron
- Jennifer
- Aaron's father

- Jennifer's mother
- Aaron's best friend
- Jennifer's best friend

You may wish to assign a character to each group or allow groups to choose a character. It will not matter if two or more groups choose the same character; there are enough variables to ensure that no two entries will be alike.

Explain to students that because they are writing diary entries, they will write from the character's point of view and should refer to the character as *I* or *me*. Have each group choose a recorder, but remind them that every member should contribute to the entry.

Suggest that groups generate ideas for the entry by brainstorming ways to complete the following sentence: "This morning I was very surprised . . . "

When students have finished writing, encourage representatives to read their group's entries. Then display the entries in the classroom.

You may wish to assign extra credit to individuals who want to write more entries for a character's diary.

Thinking Strategy

Explain to students that writing diary or journal entries help people to reflect on the day's events and to organize their thoughts. Critical thinkers from all walks of life often keep diaries or journals.

What Works

Many teachers have found that keeping diaries or journals helps students develop both their writing skills and their thinking skills. It also gives students a chance to explore ideas before sharing them with the class.

TEACHING THE LESSONS

Lesson 1: Setting Goals for the Future (pages 38–39)

Thinking Skill Objectives:

- Students will **set short-term goals.**
- Students will **set long-term goals.**

Content Objective:

- Students will learn how to write goals.

Have students read the lesson introduction on page 38. To make sure that they understand the difference between short-term goals and long-term goals, have them generate several examples similar to the math final and college-degree goals stated in the introduction.

Ask students to write their answers to questions 1–4 on page 39. Have them complete the graphic organizer on page 38 before answering questions 5–7 on page 39.

Sidenote Connection

Make students aware of the information about setting goals in the sidenotes "The Language of Thinking," "Personal Goals," and "How to Write a Goal." Explain that these sidenotes will help students to complete the graphic organizer and to answer the questions in this lesson.

Using the Graphic Organizer (page 38)

You may wish to model a response for each kind of goal on the chalkboard before students begin. Then have them continue filling in the chart individually. Point out that goals should be written according to the formula shown in the "How to Write a Goal" sidenote on page 39.

Responses (page 39)

Answers will vary.

1. Students should list their highest priority interests.
2. Students should explain what success would be for them.
3. Students should list any achievements from school, work experiences, or their personal life.
4. The skills listed should be appropriate for attaining the stated goals.
5. Steps listed should be those that would help lead to achievement of the long-term goal listed.
6. Students' explanations should detail the effects of having reached the goal.

ESL/LEP Strategy

Students from other countries may wish to include some of the following as goals:

- I will learn to speak, read, and write English fluently.
- I will return to my homeland.
- I will become a United States citizen.
- I will be reunited with my family.

Have students discuss the actions that will be needed to achieve these goals.

Thinking Journal

Ask students to explore in their Thinking Journals the steps they use to establish one of their short- or long-term goals. Some of the questions they might consider include: What should they consider before they decide to pursue this goal? What about this goal sounds attractive to them? What plans will they have to make to implement this goal? Why did they choose this goal?

Discussion (page 39)

Distribute three 3" x 5" index cards to each student. Have students prepare for the discussion by writing an answer to one of the three discussion questions on each index card. Ask students to write their names on the cards so that you can give them credit for their work later. Explain, however, that their names will not be read aloud with their answers if they write "anonymous" next to their names.

Ask a volunteer to collect answers to the first question. Have another student collect cards for the second question, and a third student collect the remaining answers.

Give the three volunteers a few minutes to sort their cards for duplicate answers. Then have the first volunteer reread the question aloud along with an answer from one of the cards. Encourage the class to discuss the answer, defending or politely opposing the writer's opinion.

Have each volunteer read five cards from his or her set. You may wish to have more answers read and discussed if time permits.

Thinking Strategy

Explain to students that critical thinkers often write their responses to questions before entering a discussion if they know beforehand what the questions will be. Writing answers first gives discussion participants a chance to organize their thoughts and explore ideas before stating them publicly.

What Works

Teachers have found that using the index-card strategy for discussions gives shy students who do not usually speak up a chance to be heard. It also allows students the opportunity to express anonymously opinions that they might otherwise feel uncomfortable stating.

Alternative to the Discussion

As an alternative to the discussion on page 39, you may wish to have students write letters to relatives or friends as a way to express their goals. Letters may cover topics brought up in the questions for discussion, such as the conflict involved when students' goals do not mesh with other people's expectations. Letters need not be sent at the end of the activity.

Evaluation Tip

Consider grading and evaluating students on one or more of the following activities in this lesson:

- responses to questions on page 38
- completion of the graphic organizer, including goals written according to the criteria in the sidenote "How to Write a Goal"
- responses that students wrote on index cards for the class-discussion
- oral participation in the class discussion
- letters students wrote as an alternative to the class discussion activity

You may wish to add the scores for the activities together to assign a grade for the lesson.

Lesson 2: Evaluating Information (pages 40–41)

Thinking Skill Objectives:

- Students will **gather** and **evaluate** information.
- Students will **clarify** their goals.
- Students will **classify** sources of information.

Content Objective:

- Students will complete a questionnaire.

Explain to students that in this lesson they will learn how to gather and evaluate the information they need to make good choices. Then ask students to read the lesson introduction on page 40, including the numbered items.

Before continuing with the lesson, you might want to check whether students have understood the information in the introduction. Invite volunteers to paraphrase each of the four points on page 40. Briefly discuss how sources that may be considered expert in one area might not be reliable in other areas or situations. A friend who knows a lot about computers, for example, may know very little about cars.

Help students list resources they could consult for information by writing a few of their responses on the chalkboard. Responses might include the following:

- relatives, friends, and teachers that students consider to be wise, knowledgeable, or expert in a field
- books and encyclopedia articles on a subject
- magazines or magazine articles on specific subjects
- salespeople and professionals

Sidenote Connection

Point out to students the definition of *evaluate* in sidenote "The Language of Thinking." Then have students read the questions that follow it. Ask students if there are any other questions that they would ask themselves when they need to evaluate information.

If you choose to use the following cooperative learning strategy, tell students to ask themselves the sidenote questions when they suggest sources in the activity.

Cooperative Learning Strategy

Divide the class into groups of four or five students. Have each member of a group use a different colored pen, marker, or pencil for this activity.

Give each group a piece of paper. Tell students to think of situations in which they would want to have reliable information before they made a decision, such as buying a car, renting an apartment, applying to a college, and buying furniture. Have each student write a situation and then pass the paper clockwise to a different member of the group. Ask students to leave space between items.

After each member has written a situation, have groups rotate the paper again, this time listing sources of information for each situation. Tell them to write sources for situations other than the one they listed. Sources can be anything from a knowledgeable uncle to *Consumer Reports* magazine. Rotate the paper one more time so that students can write a second source for each situation.

Have the group member who was the first to write a situation act as group leader. Tell the leader to read the situations one at a time to the group. Have students discuss whether the sources listed might give reliable information in the situations listed.

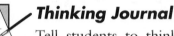 ### Thinking Journal

Tell students to think of one of the sources they cited or learned about during the Cooperative Learning Activity they have completed. They should then write in their Thinking Journals about how they would determine if this source is reliable and objective.

Completing the Questionnaire (page 41)

Before students complete the questionnaire, have them divide into pairs. Explain that each student should complete a form individually but that partners may give one another help and suggestions as they work.

You may wish to have students share their responses by writing them on the chalkboard or on a chart. Then initiate a class discussion in which you encourage students to explain why they responded as they did to each question. Remind students that there are no right or wrong answers to these questions.

Responses (page 41)

Answers will vary. Possible responses follow.

1. Students should list four cities, towns, or areas.
2. Students should write a rating in the brackets next to the place name. All four places should be listed.
3. The labels "E," "H," and "R" should be written in the brackets next to place names that were ranked 2 or 1 in the second question.

4. Students should write "E," "H," or "R" on the first line and explain their opinion of its reliability on the second line.

5. Students might state that they would need information about jobs in the area, housing, transportation, weather, or educational opportunities.

6. Students might mention such sources as books, the area's chamber of commerce, travel brochures and travel agencies, immigration services, and people who know the area.

7. Students should make realistic statements about the role of their own experience.

ESL/LEP Strategy

Invite ESL/LEP students to volunteer to be sources of information on their native countries. Ask them to talk to the class about places in their native countries. Encourage them to bring in photographs, maps, books, or any other information that might be helpful to classmates as they complete the questionnaires.

Thinking Strategy

Explain to students that answering questionnaires can help people become more aware of their own thinking processes. Completing questionnaires also helps critical thinkers make generalizations about the information they wrote for their answers.

Sidenote Connection

You may wish to offer extra credit to students who volunteer for the following activity.

Encourage students to bring to class books listed in the "Bookshelf" sidenote on page 41 or other books that deal with the topic of living independently.

Have students choose and read aloud short passages or quotations that they think the rest of the class would find interesting. Allow time for discussion of the passages and books.

Evaluation Tip

If you choose to assign grades for work in this lesson, you may wish to include students' completion of the questionnaire. Explain that students will not be graded on the alternatives they listed but on how well they evaluated their choices and information.

You may wish to explain to students how you assigned points on the questionnaires so that students

will understand how they were evaluated. Consider, also, discussing students' questionnaires during individual conferences.

Lesson 3: Prioritizing Alternatives (pages 42–43)

Thinking Skill Objectives:

- Students will **describe** a critical decision they need to make.
- Students will **identify** their alternatives.
- Students will **prioritize** their values and alternatives.

Content Objective:

- Students will learn how to use critical thinking skills when making a decision.

Have students read the lesson introduction on page 42. After they have also read the sidenote "Facts about Decisions" on page 43, divide the class into groups of three or four to discuss the sidenote. You may wish to use one or more of the following questions as discussion starters:

- How are decisions that adults are faced with different from those that children or teens make?

- Would life be different if everyone learned how to improve their decision-making skills? If yes, how? If no, why not?

- Name a difficult decision you have had to make. What was your course of action? What alternative did you choose? What was the outcome?

Cooperative Learning Strategy

Before students write their critical decisions and alternatives, you may wish to model the exercise, using a nonpersonal example. Invite a volunteer to write students' responses on the chalkboard. Ask students to name a political figure, a celebrity, or a community leader who is facing a critical decision. Then have the volunteer write on the chalkboard the critical decision that students indicated.

Next, ask the class to name at least four actions the person could take. Have the recorder list them under the critical decision. You may wish to have the class discuss the alternatives briefly and vote for the one they think the subject is most likely to choose. Have students then discuss whether that choice is the best course of action.

Sidenote Connection

Before students prioritize the values listed on page 42, suggest that they read the sidenote "The Language of Thinking." Have a volunteer paraphrase the definition of *prioritize* in the first paragraph of the sidenote. Then ask another student to summarize the information in the next two paragraphs.

Remind students that when readers paraphrase, they restate what they have read in their own words. When readers summarize, they restate in their own words the main idea of the material they read.

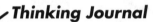

Thinking Journal

Ask students to reflect in their Thinking Journals about how prioritizing their actions can help them achieve a goal. Suggest that they think of a day in which they felt that they had too much to do. How did they impose some order on their tasks so that, at least, the most important ones were done?

Thinking Strategy

Explain to students that critical thinkers often paraphrase and summarize what they read. Both strategies can help readers understand and remember new information and ideas.

What Works

Many teachers have found that students get more out of their reading materials when they have learned strategies for extracting information and for remembering what they read.

Using the Graphic Organizer (page 43)

You may wish to have students work in pairs as they complete their charts. Students who have written critical decisions of a very personal nature, however, may prefer to work on their charts alone.

Some students, especially those from other countries, may want to add more values to the list on page 42 before completing the chart. (See the following ESL/LEP note.) Allow them to add values, such as *family* or *honor*, that they feel would affect their decision making.

Make sure students understand that the numbers assigned to alternatives do not represent a priority ranking; those numbers are used here only to differentiate among the courses of action. However, the numbers that students write next to their values *do* represent a priority ranking. Students who add values to the list on page 42 will, of course, have more numbers in their rating system.

ESL/LEP Strategy

Tell students from other countries to think about whether some values generally seem to have more or less importance here than in their homeland. Invite students to describe to the class differences they find between the two cultures' values. (Students from some countries may remark on the priority given to money and free time here, compared to the importance of family and honor in their countries.)

Point out that one culture's values should not be judged as better or worse than those of another culture, but that critical thinkers learn about and respect such differences.

Responses (page 43)

Answers will vary according to the alternatives and values listed on each student's chart.

1. Students should write one alternative. If two alternatives have the same number of values, both may be named.

2. Students should write the alternative that is paired with the highest priority values.

3. If the alternative listed for question 1 is the same as the answer for question 2, it should also be the answer for question 3. A second alternative listed for question 1 would have to be eliminated as an option after question 2 is answered.

4. Students should mention that they have a clearer understanding of what their values are and of how those values help direct their decision making.

5. Depending on the decision listed on the chart, students might name the following

sources of information: books, newspapers, magazines, or people who students consider to be experts in the field.

Evaluation Tip

You may wish to grade students on one or more of the following activities:

- their participation at the beginning of this lesson in the class discussion of "Facts about Decisions"
- their participation in the cooperative learning strategy
- their completion of the chart
- their responses to the questions on page 43

You may wish to assure students that their work will be evaluated only on how well they participated in activities or completed their work. Explain that they will not be judged on their opinions, decisions, or values.

MAKING CONNECTIONS

Preparing For Life's Decisions (pages 44–47)

Thinking Skill Objectives:

- Students will **analyze** how they spend their time.
- Students will **identify** their long-term goals.
- Students will **plan** how to achieve their goals.
- Students will **evaluate** their work.
- Students will **apply** what they learned in the unit lessons.

Content Objectives:

- Students will prepare to make important decisions about their lives.
- Students will share their work on the final project with the class.

Before students begin their unit project, have them read the project introduction on page 44. Point out that the second paragraph summarizes what they did and learned in the three unit lessons. Explain that they should apply what they have learned in the lessons as they complete each step of the final project.

Step 1: Computing Your Time Each Day (pages 44–45)

You may wish to model a pie chart on the chalkboard for students, emphasizing how the pie sections approximate in size the percentage of the pie the sections represent. Point out, for example, that a pie section representing 25 percent of a student's time should take up a fourth of the pie. A piece representing 33 percent should measure about a third of the pie.

Encourage group members with strong math skills to help other students determine percentages, if necessary.

Thinking Strategy

Explain to students that critical thinkers use pie charts in business reports, for marketing, to show medical and researcher findings, and in many other ways. Point out that people make pie charts to help themselves understand data and to communicate visually information to others. Stress that because pie charts are so widely used, knowing how to read, interpret, and make pie graphs is an essential skill today.

What Works

Many teachers have found that pie charts make data visible and concrete for all students, including those with limited language skills. But pie charts not only communicate information; they also are effective thinking organizers.

Thinking Journal

Direct students to review the graphic organizer they have constructed for Step 1 and to draw conclusions about how they spend their time during an average day. Have them reflect on what they learned about themselves. Did any of the information surprise them? How could they use this information to make their lives easier or more ordered?

Step 2: Setting Goals (pages 45–46)

If students choose to share information about their long-term goals, allow them to display their charts as transparencies, on posters, or on the chalkboard. Have them explain to the class why they included certain items in their chart. Invite class discussion after each display.

Step 3: Making a Plan (pages 46–47)

After students have written their plans, ask them to check whether they have followed the four points listed in this step. When they are satisfied with their work, invite them to share the plans in groups of five.

Cooperative Learning Strategy

Suggest that groups choose a member to act as a reporter on the group's progress. Ask the reporters to tell the class about the kinds of plans that were developed by members of their groups.

You may wish to use the following strategy for selecting group reporters. Ask each member of a group to count off, starting at one. Pick a random number from 1–5. Then have each student with that number present the group's report.

Step 4: Evaluating the Project (page 47)

You may wish to grade students on their unit project. Consider using the four points listed in Step 3 as part of your criteria. Other items that might contribute to the final score could include students' completion of the graphic organizers and their participation in both group and class discussions.

Unit Test (page 48)

In addition to, or as an alternative to, the unit project, you may wish to have students complete the unit test.

Responses

1. c. Students should mention that it is important to set goals that can be reached.

2. Students should mark the first answer and mention that it is a mistake sometimes made in decision making.

3. Answers will vary. Students should mention that thinking about long-term and short-term goals will help students to plan their futures and, therefore, to be more successful at living independently.

4. Answers will vary. Students should mention that it isn't possible to make good decisions if you aren't clear about what is important to you.

use of language on various radio shows and radio commercials.

Encourage groups to make a mural, collage, or other display of poignant articles, cartoons, lyrics, advertisements, transcripts of radio or television propaganda, and so on.

Explain that this is an ongoing project that students can work on as they complete the unit. You may wish to have groups report on their findings at specific intervals, such as at the end of each lesson, or whenever they find an item that particularly interests them.

What Works

Many teachers have found that they are more successful teaching thinking strategies when they give groups of students the opportunity to discuss and reflect on the mechanics and uses of the strategy.

UNIT 4

Don't Believe Everything You See and Hear

BEGINNING THE UNIT

Unit Introduction (page 49)

Engaging the Students

After students have read the unit introduction on page 49, tell them that in this unit they are going to think critically about how the mass media influences them.

Begin by dividing the class into five groups. Explain that the class will be examining the impact of all media on society, but that each group will be responsible for a more detailed inspection of one medium. Then assign one of the following to each group: film; television; radio and recordings; newspapers and magazines; and textbooks and trade books.

Appoint a leader for each group. Tell the leaders to assign subtopics for group members to research and report on to the group or class. Suggestions for subtopics may be generated by all group members.

An individual in the "radio and recordings" group, for example, might explore the use of radio by political groups, while another student might research the ways rap music has affected society. A third student in that group might survey the use and mis-

Thinking Strategy

Explain to students that in a democracy, the mass media is expected to be a watchdog for society—constantly reporting the workings of their government. Critical thinkers, however, must train themselves to be watchdogs of the mass media and not allow the media to do their thinking for them. Critical thinkers constantly ask themselves questions about what they read, hear, and see in the media.

Seeing Shouldn't Be Believing (pages 50–52)

Ask students to read the short story, "Seeing Shouldn't Be Believing." Then invite them to write questions about the story. You may wish to have them work in pairs for this activity.

The following are examples of questions students might generate. Consider listing several of these questions on the chalkboard to help students get started or to add to their lists:

1. What is the theme of the story? (Stereotyping is offensive.)

2. What did Erica dislike about "My Life"? (She disliked the sexual stereotyping.)

3. Should people write letters of complaint about shows with offensive stereotyping? To whom should the letters be directed? (Letters can and should be written to networks, the FCC, and commercial sponsors of shows.)

4. Why is it important to think critically about television shows? (If we do not think critically about television, we may be easily manipulated in our thinking and our actions.)

ESL/LEP Strategy

Invite ESL/LEP students to share with the class details about television shows in their native countries. Have the rest of the class ask questions about similarities and differences in television viewing in other countries and in the United States. Ask ESL/LEP students to cite examples of stereotyping on television shows in their native countries.

Have ESL/LEP students pair up with members of the rest of the class to make Venn diagrams showing likenesses and differences between television viewing here and abroad.

TEACHING THE LESSONS

Lesson 1: Distinguishing Between Fact and Opinion (pages 53–55)

Thinking Skill Objectives:

- Students will **identify** the qualities of facts.
- Students will **identify** the qualities of opinions.
- Students will **distinguish** between statements that are facts and statements that are opinions.
- Students will **read critically** to **distinguish** between facts and opinions.

Content Objective:

- Students will learn the value and uses of both facts and opinions.

Ask students to read the introduction to Lesson 1 on page 53. Encourage the five groups formed at the beginning of this unit to think critically about the use of fact and opinion in the medium they are covering: radio and recordings, television, film, magazines and newspapers, or textbooks and trade books.

You may wish to have students discuss the quotations on page 53 in pairs or small groups before they label them as facts or opinions.

Responses (pages 53–54)

1. Opinion
2. Opinion
3. Fact
4. Opinion
5. Opinion

Thinking Strategy

Explain to students that when critical thinkers read or hear quotations from famous people, they look for a propaganda technique called *testimonial.*

Advertisers and political groups often hire or enlist famous people to persuade others to buy something or join a cause. Critical thinkers realize that such testimonials can be misleading and that a product or cause is not necessarily good just because a celebrity says it is.

What Works

Many teachers have found that when students are taught to recognize propaganda techniques, such as testimonials, they are better able to distinguish between fact and opinion in advertising.

Sidenote Connection

Before students answer the questions on page 54, have them read the sidenotes "Checking Facts" and "Facts in the Almanac." Challenge students with one or more of the following activities:

- Bring to class several almanacs, some world and some more specific, published by various companies. Have students compare the kinds of information found in them.

- After students have named the sources they would use to check the statements on page 54, have them turn to those sources to see if they were correct.

- Have individuals or pairs of students use almanacs to check the facts listed in the "Facts in the Almanac" sidenote. Ask them to report their findings to the class.

Responses (page 54)

1. F, encyclopedia or a *Who's Who*
2. O, The stars on the flag represent the fifty states and the stripes honor the original thirteen colonies.
3. F, encyclopedia or almanac
4. F, encyclopedia or a *Who's Who*
5. O, Many Americans read *People* magazine.
6. F, newspaper or a department of commerce brochure

Cooperative Learning Strategy

Distribute two envelopes to each student. Tell them to write a fact on the front of one envelope and an opinion on the other. Shuffle the envelopes and redistribute them to students, making sure that envelopes are not returned to their senders.

Have students write on a slip of paper whether they think the statement is a fact or an opinion. Tell them to also write a brief explanation of their response and to tuck their answers in the envelopes.

Collect the envelopes. Call on volunteers to read the fact or opinion on several envelopes along with the responses inside. Allow the class to discuss whether they agree with the responses.

If you plan to grade students on this activity, be sure to have senders write their names on the envelopes and receivers write their names on the slips of paper.

Discussion (page 55)

Challenge several students to restate the focus of the discussion in their own words. You may wish to have pairs or small groups of students brainstorm answers to the questions in the text.

Remind students to think about how advertisers use testimonials to sell products.

Alternative to the Discussion

Instead of using the discussion question on page 55, you may wish to conduct the following activity. Divide students into groups of three. Tell each group to create a three-page travel brochure for a place of their choice. Have each group member write one page of the brochure.

The first page of the brochure should contain only opinions about the place. The second page should use facts exclusively, and the third page should include a mix of fact and opinion. Encourage students to use almanacs and encyclopedias to check their facts.

Evaluation Tip

You may wish to evaluate students by awarding one point for each fact they listed in the graphic organizer that adequately supports their opinion. Award an extra point for a clearly written opinion, for a maximum of five points.

Lesson 2: Comparing the Emotional Effect of Words (pages 56–57)

Thinking Skill Objectives:

- Students will **identify** words that have positive or neutral associations and those that have negative associations.
- Students will **compare** the emotional impact positive and negative words can have.
- Students will **make judgments** about the use and misuse of language.

Content Objective:

- Students will practice using critical thinking to detect doublespeak and other misuses of language.

Have students read the lesson introduction on page 56. Then suggest that the five groups, formed at the beginning of the unit, study the medium they are covering for the use of words with positive or negative associations. Tell them to examine the use of language in as many aspects of their medium as possible. The television group, for example, might look at the way positive and negative words have been incorporated into TV commentaries, commercials, interviews, sit-coms, game shows, news broadcasts, and even public-service announcements.

ESL/LEP Strategy

Before comparing word meanings on the graphic organizer, offer extra help to ESL/LEP students in one or more of the following ways:

- Pair ESL/LEP students with individuals who have strong language skills.

- Make sure each ESL/LEP student has access to a thesaurus and knows how to use it.
- Check that each ESL/LEP student has both an English dictionary and a dictionary with definitions written in the student's native language and English.

Using the Graphic Organizer (page 57)

You may wish to have students complete the graphic organizer individually or in small groups. Students should complete the organizer in the following way.

Negative words:

1. scrawny, bony, skeletal
2. smell, stink, odor
3. stubborn, pig-headed, obstinate
4. fanatic, conceited, arrogant

Positive words:

1. thin, slender, slim
2. scent, aroma, fragrance
3. determined, unflinching, steadfast
4. confident, unhesitating, certain

Sidenote Connection

Before students complete the doublespeak activity on page 57, have them read the "Doublespeak and Euphemisms" sidenote on page 56. Encourage every student to bring to class either:

- one example of doublespeak or a euphemism found in print, or
- an example of a euphemism or doublespeak they heard on television, radio, a recording, or in film.

Invite students to read their passages aloud and involve the class in a discussion of the associations and hidden meanings in each excerpt.

Responses (page 57)

1. failure
2. taxes
3. death
4. prison

Thinking Strategy

Explain to students that critical thinkers are not fooled or mislead by doublespeak when they read or hear it. Critical readers and listeners analyze doublespeak to reveal the true meaning behind the words.

Euphemisms, on the other hand, are sometimes used by critical thinkers themselves when it is important to state information gently. Critical thinkers are careful to spare other people's feelings.

Thinking Journal

Have students distinguish in their Thinking Journals between appropriate and inappropriate times to use euphemisms. They should contrast euphemisms that are meant to spare a person's feelings with those that are meant to hide a person's real intentions.

What Works

Many teachers have found that using euphemisms in the classroom is an acceptable way to convey constructive criticism. Euphemisms can be especially helpful in peer editing situations and in group discussions. Remind students of the old adage, "You can catch more flies with honey than with vinegar."

Evaluation Tip

Have small groups list up to five examples of doublespeak and euphemisms, with their meanings, that they have seen or heard. They should present their lists to the class. You might award groups one point for each example they offer.

Lesson 3: Identifying Sexist Language and Stereotypes (pages 58–59)

Thinking Skill Objectives:

- Students will **identify** stereotyping.
- Students will **identify** sexist language.
- Students will **make judgments** about the implications of language.

Content Objective:

- Students will learn how to correct sexist language.

Explain to students that this lesson has two purposes:

- to help them become aware of two of the most harmful misuses of language, stereotyping and sexist phrasing, and
- to show them how they can rephrase sexist language and stereotypes.

After students have read the introduction to Lesson 3, ask volunteers to paraphrase the definition of stereotyping given in the first sentence of the introduction. You may wish to have them briefly discuss the harm that can be done by stereotyping before they respond to the activity on page 58. Remind them, too, to look for sexist language and stereotyping in the media the groups are investigating: television, film, radio and recordings, newspapers and magazines, and textbooks and trade books.

Responses (page 58)

Answers will vary.

1. The statement implies that people of Irish descent have quick tempers.
2. This statement suggests that males should not express their feelings.
3. The stereotype here is that intelligent people are serious and boring.
4. This headline implies that the candidate is not qualified for the office.
5. These sentences stereotype all politicians as untrustworthy and do not respect the person's individuality.

ESL/LEP Strategy

After students read about the use of *he* and *him* at the bottom of page 58, explain that some languages do not have the same pronoun difficulties that English has. In Turkish, for example, the neuter pronoun *o* helps speakers and writers avoid some of the awkward situations that crop up in English. On the other hand, some languages, including Spanish and French, assign a gender to most nouns.

Invite ESL/LEP students to tell the class about the use of gender in their native languages. Ask them how, and if, pronouns are used in their native languages. Have them explain if this issue is discussed in their native country.

Sidenote Connection

Before students correct the sexist words on page 59, have them read the "Correcting Sexist Language" sidenote on page 58. Tell them to also read the sidenote "The Matter of Ms." on page 59 at this time.

You may wish to have students work in small groups as they do the activities on page 59. Check that each group has access to a thesaurus or dictionary.

Responses (page 59)

Answers will vary.

1. Students may suggest that *actor,* or *star* can refer to members of either sex.
2. Students may offer *workers,* and *police officer* as alternatives.
3. Students may suggest *humankind* to refer to people.
4. *Women* could be a preferable term.

Answers will vary.

1. *prehistoric men and women* or *prehistoric people*
2. *chairperson* or *chair*
3. *an application* or *his or her application*; *Ms. Gray*
4. *Let's each pay our own way.*

Cooperative Learning Strategy

Divide the class into several groups. Have each group choose a document or passage that was written before the 1970s. The *Declaration of Independence, Gettysburg Address,* and the lyrics to traditional songs are possible choices.

Tell students to rewrite sexist words and phrases and to remove other stereotypes in the excerpts.

Have a representative from each group read the original passage and another student read the group's revision.

Thinking Strategy

Explain to students that the use of sexist language in masterpieces such as the *Declaration of Independence* and the *Gettysburg Address* does not detract from the importance or elegance of these documents. Explain that before the 1970s, most people were not sensitive to sexist language.

Tell students that critical thinkers keep in perspective the ideas and concerns of the era in which a piece was written and make allowances for the different ways that people think about language.

What Works

Many teachers have found that giving students a chance to discuss and reflect upon stereotyping through a cooperative learning activity can help students become sensitive to hurtful language.

It is important, however, to help students understand that different eras had different concerns.

Discussion (page 59)

For this activity, you may wish to divide the class into groups and assign each group one of the discussion questions.

Have each group brainstorm aspects of the question before they formulate a response. Each response should consist of a main opinion statement that students support with facts and details.

You may want to suggest that each group appoint a recorder to take the group's dictation for both the brainstorming and the formal response. The group may then appoint a reporter to read the response to the class.

Alternative to the Discussion

As an alternative to the Discussion on page 59, you may wish to have all or part of the class read and report on books about people who have fought against stereotyping.

You may want to allow students to choose books themselves in libraries or from other sources. The following are books you might recommend to students who do not have strong reading skills. The interest level is high, but students will not find them excessively challenging.

- *Amos Fortune, Free Man* by Elizabeth Yates. This Newbery Medal winner is a novel about a former slave who broke through stereotypes about African Americans to become a successful business person.
- *Journey to Topas* by Yoshiko Uchida. This novel explores the experiences of Japanese Americans who were stereotyped as enemies and sent to internment camps during World War II.
- *The New Immigrants* by Carol Olsen Day and Edmund Day. Students can read about the difficulties faced by Asian, Caribbean, and Latin American immigrants in the United States.

Evaluation Tip

Consider evaluating and grading students on the work they have done up to now for the mass media group assignments made at the beginning of this unit. You might want to grade the work completed by each group and use that grade as part of each member's complete grade for the activity. The rest of each student's grade might be based on work done individually for the group activity.

Explain to students that though they are being evaluated on their media group work now, they should be sure to save their work in order to apply it to their unit projects.

MAKING CONNECTIONS

Reporting the News: "Language Abuse Exposed!" (pages 60–63)

Thinking Skill Objectives:

- Students will **plan** the steps they will take to uncover language abuse in the media.
- Students will **gather** facts and examples of how language is misused in the media.
- Students will **select** the information and examples they will present.
- Students will **prioritize** sources.
- Students will **analyze** ways in which the media uses language.
- Students will **evaluate** each other's projects.

Content Objectives:

- Students will assemble group presentations about the misuse of language.
- Students will present their findings in a mock news broadcast.

Before you assign the unit project, have three volunteers summarize the material explored in this unit. Have each volunteer cover one of the three lessons.

Then ask students to read the introduction to the project on page 60. As you discuss the final project with the class, ask them how they might apply what they have learned in the unit lessons to the project.

Cooperative Learning Strategy

Allow the media groups that were established at the beginning of the unit to meet and discuss what they learned about language use and misuse in the media they have been researching. Explain that they should now pool their findings into a Class Media Library so that the information they have gathered can be used by all students as they complete the unit project.

You may wish to have students complete the unit project by working within their media groups. Or you may wish to form new groups with five members each, so that each group has a mix of media backgrounds.

Step 1: Brainstorming and Planning (pages 61–62)

Before students begin planning their broadcasts, you may wish to have them watch one or more television news programs. If you have access to a school television, consider taping excerpts from a few news broadcasts and playing them in the classroom. Initiate a class discussion about various aspects of the broadcast and the job of the reporter.

Using the Graphic Organizer (page 61)

You may want to model one or two responses for students on the chalkboard or on a transparency. Then allow students to complete the cluster maps individually.

What Works

Many teachers have found that the cluster map is one of the most useful tools for critical thinking. It allows students to organize their thoughts quickly. In addition, suggest that students use a highlighter to select and remember important data.

Thinking Journal

Tell students to reflect in their Thinking Journals about how they might use a cluster map to help them organize their information on other projects or class assignments.

Thinking Strategy

Explain to students that in this step they are applying several thinking strategies that they have learned.

1. They are using the cluster map as a vehicle for recording the ideas they brainstorm.
2. They are identifying in their charts the most likely sources of language misuse.
3. They are prioritizing their choices.

Explain that critical thinkers often use strategies in combinations like this when they plan projects or solve problems.

Step 2: Gathering Facts and Examples (pages 61–62)

In this step, students will gather examples of language misuse in the media. Remind them to look at the materials gathered in the Class Media Library for examples and facts.

You may want to display a list of the students who researched each medium so the class knows whom to ask for information.

ESL/LEP Strategy

You may want to assign each ESL/LEP student a project partner for work on the unit project. The partner could be a speaker of the student's native language who is also fluent in English.

Remind partners to speak slowly and clearly, but without exaggerating sounds; to explain unfamiliar terms; and to clarify slang, idioms, and contractions.

Step 3: Planning a Presentation (page 62)

Explain to students that program managers post the contents and schedules of news shows so that everyone knows which reporter will be giving which report and when. Have groups create a chart to help them prepare written schedules for their broadcasts. When titles for presentations have been determined, have groups add that information as well.

Step 4: Rehearsing (page 63)

Give each group as much privacy as possible for rehearsing their broadcasts. If available, unoccupied rooms or areas other than the classroom could be used.

Remind group members to offer encouragement, as well as suggestions for improvement, as they watch others rehearse. Advise students, too, to try out any audiovisual material during the rehearsal so that they can determine how well their props and aids work.

What Works

Many teachers have found that when groups have the responsibility and an interest in making sure everyone in the group is prepared, presentations and productions usually run more smoothly. In this strategy, peer pressure is applied in a constructive way.

Step 5: Broadcasting the News (page 63)

You may wish to spread the broadcasts out over several days. If so, ask each group to contribute its listings and have group representatives coordinate the presentations into a class schedule. The representatives could use a typewriter or computer to make the final schedule look like a real program guide. If possible, make copies of the schedule and distribute them to the class.

Consider presenting the broadcast to one or more additional classes at your school. If you decide to invite other students, you may wish to provide them with schedules, too. It might be wise to have an in-class broadcast before opening it up to a wider audience.

Step 6: Evaluating Your Presentation (page 63)

You may wish to allow students to participate in the evaluation of the unit project. If so, consider having students write reviews of the broadcasts. The reviews themselves can then be evaluated by you.

For this activity, bring to class a few reviews of television programs from newspapers, magazines, and television guides so that students can see the formats used.

Cooperative Learning Strategy

As an alternative to having students write reviews, consider the following checklist strategy as a way of involving students in the evaluation of the unit project.

As each group gives its broadcast, have the audience (class members only) answer the questions below. Allow time for students to write their responses after each broadcast.

1. Was the broadcast clear and understandable?
2. Did it hold the attention of the audience?
3. Was the presentation informative about the abuses of language?
4. Did it want to make you learn more about the topic?
5. Did the report seem well researched?

Unit Test (page 64)

In addition to, or as an alternative to, the unit project, you may wish to have students complete the unit test.

Responses

1. a. sexist language. Women now are included when speaking of all people.

   b. stating opinion as fact. Others may prefer different breeds.

   c. promoting stereotypes. Assumes that English people are dull.

2. Students should state that people who are not able to distinguish opinions from facts can be easily mislead or tricked.

3. Students should describe a society in which citizens do not harm each other with misuses of language.

Becoming a Smarter Consumer

BEGINNING THE UNIT

Unit Introduction (page 65)

Engaging the Students

After students have read the unit introduction on page 65, explain that con artists are masters at using persuasion to involve people in scams and frauds. Tell students that con artists know what is important to people. They know people's weak spots, and they make their appeals to those vulnerabilities.

Have students discuss how each of the following wishes could become a target for a con artist: Many people wish to save money, be socially accepted, become or remain healthy, keep their family safe, get a good education, and travel or enjoy vacation time. Invite students to create scenarios for each situation and to add to the "wish list."

Thinking Strategy

Explain to students that critical thinkers know that there is nothing wrong with using persuasion as long as there is no fraudulent intent.

To protect themselves, however, good critical thinkers try to always be aware of three things:

- their vulnerabilities, which may leave them open to persuasion and even to scams
- persuasive techniques that others may be using
- the effect of their actions

Critical thinkers want to know when they are being persuaded, by whom, and for what reason.

Are You Gullible? (pages 66–68)

Before students complete the questionnaire, tell them to ask themselves the question, "Would I fall victim to a con artist's scheme?" Then have students complete the questionnaire independently.

When students have completed and scored their questionnaires, have them read "Where to Go for Help." Ask which services they could contact about the schemes in the questionnaire.

What Works

Many teachers have found that students get the most out of questionnaires when they try to predict their scores and to draw conclusions.

Cooperative Learning Strategy

Divide the class into pairs or small groups to complete the questionnaire. Encourage students to discuss the options before choosing an answer. Tell them to look for patterns and commonalties among the four choices. Challenge them to draw conclusions about their scores before they read "Scoring Your Answers" and "Behind the Schemes" on page 67.

Allow groups to decide whether they want to publicize their gullibility quotients or keep the information to themselves.

Thinking Strategy

Explain to students that predicting scores or outcomes on questionnaires can help people sharpen their metacognitive skills. Questionnaires allow people to think about *what* they think and about *how* they think.

TEACHING THE LESSONS

Lesson 1: Identifying Deceptive Practices (pages 69–70)

Thinking Skill Objectives:

- Students will **identify** faulty arguments and illogical reasoning.

- Students will **recognize** deceptive consumer practices.
- Students will **distinguish** between valid and deceptive practices.

Content Objective:

- Students will learn the mechanics of the pyramid scheme and "free" merchandise scams.

Have students read the lesson introduction and the mechanics of the pyramid scam on page 69. Then explain that the con artists who start pyramids rely on people not perceiving the faulty cause-and-effect relationship in the pyramid scheme. People assume that because they put their names on the list, they will receive the money.

Cooperative Learning Strategy

The following activity will help students sharpen their ability to analyze cause-and-effect relationships.

Have one or two volunteers help you tear small pieces of paper that can be put in a hat or bowl. Make enough papers for each student and write "faulty" on one-third of them. Pass the hat and tell students to keep what is on their paper secret.

On the chalkboard, write the following starter sentences:

Because it rained all week, the river overflowed.

Because the river overflowed, the bridge fell down.

Because the bridge fell down . . . .

Have students take turns giving the next sentences. (They do not need to be written on the chalkboard.) Tell them to give a logical effect for each preceding cause, unless they hold a paper that says "faulty." Faulty answers could be something like: "Because the bridge was rebuilt, it snowed the next day."

Tell students that whenever someone gives a faulty answer, the class should call out "faulty."

ESL/LEP Strategy

Immigrants, tourists, and visitors from other countries sometimes are targets of scams in the United States. Ask ESL/LEP students if they are familiar with scams that are aimed particularly at foreigners. They may tell about friends and family who have been charged too much for taxi rides, meals at restaurants, and hotel rooms. They may also tell about people who have been duped into paying for unusable real estate.

Thinking Strategy

Explain to students that good critical thinkers are cautious about offers of free goods or services from strangers. As thoughtful, critical consumers, they realize that merchants and tradespeople need to make a profit from sales of their merchandise or work. Before they accept free merchandise, critical thinkers ask themselves, "Why is this being offered to me at no cost?" Sometimes the offer is a legitimate advertising technique to get consumers acquainted with a product or service. Sometimes it is a scam.

Responses (page 70)

Pyramid Scam

1. Students should multiply the 125 people by $5.00 to arrive at $625.00.

2. Students may mention that there is no guarantee that anyone will send money to someone on the list, even if that person has sent money to someone else.

3. Answers will vary. Students may mention buying "vacation" land in a distant place that is really a swamp, or other such schemes.

Book Scam

1. The person paid $15.00.

2. Students should state that the victim did not question why the merchandise was free and did not bother to count the change at the time it was given.

3. Answers will vary. Students may mention schemes that target consumers who are in a rush or who are laden with packages. Con artists rely on busy consumers not checking their receipts before paying with cash or signing credit cards.

Thinking Journal

Direct students to write in their Thinking Journals about a time when they, or someone they know, received a chain letter or similar pyramid scam. Did they send the letters they were directed to send? How many letters did they then receive? If they did not send the letters, why did they make that decision? Finally, have students analyze why pyramid schemes are deceptive.

Evaluation Tip

Consider asking small groups to write another scenario for the free book scheme or the pyramid scam in which the targeted person recognizes the scam and is not cheated. The class could rate the groups' work on a scale of 1 to 5, in its analysis of the situation and invention of useful strategies to respond to it.

Lesson 2: Analyzing Telephone Scams (pages 71–73)

Thinking Skill Objectives:

- Students will **identify** telephone scams and **recognize** them as different from ordinary telephone sales calls.
- Students will **analyze** telephone scams.

Content Objective:

- Students will learn how to avoid becoming victims of telephone scams.

After students have read the unit introduction on page 71, have them form groups to brainstorm answers to the three questions about telephone scams. Encourage anyone who has received a scam call to tell the group about the yak's techniques.

Responses (page 71)

Answers will vary.

1. The purpose is to cheat people.
2. Students might say that victims can be swindled more than once because they keep trying to regain their original losses.
3. Students might suggest that people want to believe that others will be kind to them or will give them gifts.

Cooperative Learning Strategy

Divide the class into pairs to role-play the telephone scam script on page 72.

Allow students time to read and think about the script and the questions that follow. Then have pairs decide who will be the yak and who will be the potential victim in a remake of the scam script.

Students should think about what they have learned as they act out the script. Students who play the parts of would-be mooches should listen to the yak, but not allow themselves to be cheated. Instead, they could do one or more of the following:

- refuse to give credit card numbers over the phone
- ask for something to be mailed to them
- ask why they have been picked to win a prize if they did not enter a contest
- ask why they need to purchase transportation if they have won a free trip
- ask for the caller's phone number so that they can call him or her back when they've thought it over

Invite pairs to perform their skits for the class.

What Works

Many teachers have found that students often digest and reflect on concepts better when they are able to role-play situations that involve those concepts.

Thinking Journal

Have students write in their Thinking Journals about a time they were involved in a role-playing activity. Ask them to think about what they learned by trying to take another person's point of view. Did it give them insights into the person's thoughts? Did it help them take a more objective viewpoint?

Responses (page 72)

Answers will vary.

1. Students may mention phrases that the yak used to make it sound exciting: "all-expense-paid vacation" and "you don't have to do anything or visit any place."
2. Students should mention the credit card number.
3. Students should state that it is unlikely that the person went on the vacation and that the yak probably used the person's credit card number.

Thinking Strategy

Explain that critical thinkers are always cautious when they are asked to give personal information of any kind to strangers. When an unknown caller asks for credit card, bank account, or social security card numbers, critical thinkers tell the caller that they do not give out that information over a telephone. Critical thinkers always evaluate situations carefully before giving anyone personal information.

Responses (page 73)

Answers will vary.

1. Students should state that the yak appealed to the victim's desire to cooperate with an authority.
2. The mistake the victim made was giving the number over the telephone.
3. The victim should have asked for the caller's name, then called the phone company and asked to speak to the caller. If the caller was not an employee at the phone company, the call should have been reported as a scam.
4. Students should state that the yak appealed to the victim's desire to win a prize.
5. The mistake was giving the credit card number to the yak.
6. The victim should have told the yak that he or she would be delighted to receive the prize, but since it is free, the shipping should be free, too.

Using the Graphic Organizer (page 73)

You may wish to have students brainstorm tips for the chart before they write their individual charts. If students brainstorm as a class, you may want to have a volunteer write their tips on the chalkboard. If they brainstorm in groups, a recorder for each group could write the tips on a poster.

Evaluation Tip

Consider including reports on books and other print materials suggested in the "Bookshelf" sidenote when evaluating and grading students in this lesson. You might also evaluate students on their responses to questions, participation in discussions and role-playing, and completion of the graphic organizer.

Lesson 3: Recognizing Fraud (pages 74–75)

Thinking Skill Objectives:

- Students will **identify** fraud.
- Students will **distinguish** between fraudulent intent and legitimate sales efforts.

Content Objective:

- Students will learn how to avoid scams.

Before students separate into groups to discuss and answer the questions on page 74, have them read the definition of fraud and the introduction to Lesson 3 on that page.

Responses (page 74)

Answers will vary.

1. In a fraudulent situation there is either no land for sale or the land in uninhabitable. If the sale is legitimate, a contract for purchase of the land will be executed.
2. If the offer is fraudulent, no product is received and the victim loses the money. If the offer is legitimate, the product will be received in four to eight weeks.

Thinking Strategy

Explain to students that critical thinkers analyze sales situations carefully to distinguish cons from legitimate sales efforts. Critical thinkers ask themselves what the intent of the sales really is.

ESL/LEP Strategy

To make sure ESL/LEP students have mastered content words in this unit, ask them to write a sentence for each part of speech of each word listed in the "Fraud Vocabulary" sidenote on page 74. For the word *cheat*, for example, they should write a sentence about *a cheat*, and a sentence using the verb, *to cheat*.

Before ESL/LEP students write vocabulary sentences, you may wish to have all members of the class participate in giving verbal definitions of the words in the list, including parts of speech in parentheses.

Cooperative Learning Strategy

To reinforce recognition of frauds and legitimate sales efforts, have students play Con Concentration. First, divide the class into groups of five or six and give each student two index cards. Have students write a fraud on one card and a similar but legitimate situation on the other card. One card, for example, could describe a fraudulent "diamond" ring sale, and the other card could depict a legitimate sale.

Have one group member shuffle the completed cards and deal them face down on a desk or table. Tell the dealers to turn cards over as members try to match fraudulent situations with similar but legitimate situations. Students can win points for every match they make; the highest score wins.

What Works

Many teachers have found that game-like strategies can reinforce skills and concepts that are part of a lesson. Not only do games make learning fun, but for some students the variation in modality aids the learning process itself.

Sidenote Connection

Before students begin the activity on page 75, have them read the "Avoiding Scams and Frauds" sidenote on page 75. Suggest that they use the information in that sidenote as they complete the activity on that page. You may wish to have students respond individually or in pairs.

Responses (page 75)

Answers will vary.

1. Students should suggest getting information on the cleaning service beforehand, reading the fine print in any service contracts, refusing to be pressured into paying for a service not agreed upon, or agreeing in writing on a price beforehand.

2. Students might advise that the homeowners investigate home inspection companies before hiring one, refuse to be pressured into paying for services, get a second opinion, call other repair companies for estimates, demand to see licenses, or insist on a written warrantee.

3. Students should state that money should only be given to known charities. Unfamiliar charities should be investigated before making donations to them.

4. Students may advise the consumer to make certain that the money is going to a legitimate school, club, or group, even if part of the proceeds will pay for students' trip or education. A check for the exact amount of the subscription should be made out to the school, club, or group, and a receipt should be collected. If there is any question, the consumer should phone the organization before making out the check.

Thinking Journal

Have students imagine that someone offers them a free car, vacation, or other large gift. Tell them to write in their Thinking Journals how they will analyze the caller's offer. What questions will they ask the caller? What thinking strategies will they use to determine whether or not the offer is fraudulent?

Evaluation Tip

If you wish to grade students on their work in this lesson, you might have them write the answers to the questions in the "Evaluation" box. Grade their responses based on their use of critical thinking strategies in analyzing the situations and applying their knowledge to their everyday life.

MAKING CONNECTIONS

Reporting A Community Scam (pages 76–79)

Thinking Skill Objectives:

- Students will **research** their community's experiences with fraudulent schemes.
- Students will **generate** questionnaires about frauds in the community.
- Students will **summarize** the information they gather.
- Students will **evaluate** community scams.

Content Objectives:

- Students will plan and rehearse reports on scams in their community.
- Students will report a scam and reveal the con artist(s) behind the scheme.

Begin preparing for the final project by having students summarize what they have learned in Unit 5. As you discuss the preparations for the reports with the class, ask how what they have learned in the unit lessons might be applied to their projects. Then ask students to read the introduction to "Reporting a Community Scam" on page 76.

Assign each student to a group for the project. Then advise each group to prepare for the project by creating a class office. Suggest that they bring to class one or more large cardboard or plastic boxes to store project materials and information. Encourage them to create a filing system for notes, sources, questionnaires, report ideas, and other items. Suggest that groups keep an "open door" policy to allow groups to exchange ideas and data.

Step 1: Getting Organized (pages 76–77)

In this step, groups will identify specific sources of information about scams in their community. Questions 1–4 have been designed to help students generate source ideas. In addition to having students answer the questions, you may wish to use the following activity to help them share ideas for sources.

Cooperative Learning Strategy

Have students brainstorm individually to generate sources of information about community scams. Then have the entire class stand up. Ask one student to give a source, such as the local police department. Tell students with the same source to sit down.

Invite another student to share his or her idea for a source and have students with similar ideas sit down. Do allow, however, for variations on sources. For example, one student may suggest recent local newspapers, and another student may think of looking in libraries for newspapers from previous months.

This activity is effective for helping students exchange ideas and for saving valuable classroom time. Time is saved because every student does not need to speak, even though many ideas are being shared.

Thinking Strategy

Explain to students that when critical thinkers report on a subject, they gather information from many sources, including personal experiences, interviews with experts, print and nonprint library resources, and local newspapers.

Step 2: Writing a Questionnaire (page 77)

In this step, students will use a questionnaire to gather information. Advise students to use what they learned about questionnaires in the beginning of this unit as they develop their own questions.

Suggest that groups designate one person to make the phone calls to set up appointments, and another person to write notes afterward, thanking citizens for their participation in the group's project. Recommend that students interview in pairs.

ESL/LEP STRATEGY

Ask ESL/LEP students to volunteer the aid of their bilingual skills to groups, if people to be interviewed

will include speakers of other languages. Having an ESL/LEP student serve as a bilingual representative for a group both aids the group in its work on the project and gives the ESL/LEP student a position of importance in the group.

Step 3: Summarizing Your Information (page 78)

Depending on how many questionnaires have been filled out, groups may want to give each of their members a certain number of questionnaires or items from the questionnaires to summarize.

Using the Graphic Organizer (page 78)

You may wish to have groups copy their diagrams on the chalkboard or on posters so that the information can be shared easily with the class.

Encourage a spokesperson from each group to use the diagram as a vehicle to summarize the information gathered up to this point. Invite students to share specific strategies and questions they used on their forms, as well as comments on the information they have gathered.

What Works

Many teachers have found that cluster diagrams are excellent tools for helping students sort, categorize, and summarize information they have gathered for reports and other projects.

Step 4: Planning a Report (pages 78–79)

In this step, groups will focus on the topic of their report by completing the sentence, "Our scam report will be on _____."

Students will then role-play and rehearse the parts they will play in the presentation. Tell students that as each member is practicing, other members should take notes on elements to discuss later.

Thinking Strategy

Explain to students that focusing on a well researched and carefully selected topic helps critical thinkers give cohesiveness to reports they make.

Mention that whether they are presenting their reports to business associates, fellow students, or a television audience, critical thinkers rehearse their oral reports before presenting them.

Step 5: Presenting the Report (page 79)

If possible, arrange to have students present their reports to the school and invite regional newspapers and local television and radio stations to the presentations. Check that students have their facts correct before any accusations are made.

If more than one group will be giving a report, you may want to appoint an anchorperson to introduce, pace, and moderate the presentations.

What Works

Many teachers have found that they can help students give successful oral reports by encouraging students:

1. to select and focus on a topic, making sure that details in the report relate to the topic, and
2. to rehearse their presentations.

Step 6: Evaluating Your Report (page 79)

To help students evaluate classmates' projects, you may wish to modify the checklist of criteria in Step 4 by changing the word "we" to "the group" and adding a short write-on line in place of the bullet. Distribute the edited checklist.

After each report, allow the class time to complete the checklist. Tell students to score each item on the list with a 1, 2, or 3. A 3 should represent "done exceptionally well," a 2 would mean "satisfactory," and a 1 would represent "not done adequately."

Unit Test (page 80)

In addition to, or as an alternative to, the unit project, you may wish to have students complete the unit test.

Responses

1. b. Students may cite the definition of fraud in their explanation.

2. Both statements are true. Critical thinkers are aware of the world around them, but when they meet a new situation, they use their skills to analyze it.

3. Answers will vary, but students should mention skills, strategies, and information about scams that they have learned in this unit.

4. Answers will vary. Students should identify some of the ways senior citizens are vulnerable, such as their medical needs or possible loneliness. Suggestions may include volunteer and consumer education services.

Advise students to make copies of information they donate to the Volunteer Resource Center. Tell the class, however, that materials from the files should be looked at, copied if necessary, and promptly returned to the appropriate files. The Volunteer Resource Center should be used as a reference library, not a lending library.

UNIT 6

Teen Volunteers

BEGINNING THE UNIT

Unit Introduction (page 81)

Engaging the Students

After students have read the unit introduction on page 81, help them start a Volunteer Resource Center that they can use for unit activities and projects.

Bring to class several storage boxes and file folders. Tell students that they will collect materials that can be shared by all members of the class while they work on this unit. Encourage students to set up files and to donate the following materials:

- Reviews and lists of books on volunteering. Advise students to categorize books by the kind of volunteer work they cover.

- Descriptions or summaries of volunteer work students have already done. Ask students to share details about the jobs. Have them include names, dates, and addresses.

- Names of volunteers. If volunteers would agree to be interviewed, their phone numbers should be included.

- Volunteer services in the community. Students should note how they heard about the work and list names, addresses, and phone numbers.

What Works

Many teachers have found that having an in-class resource center where students can research current activities and projects is an important motivational tool, as well as a valuable information source.

Reaching Out: Helping the Homeless (pages 82–83)

Have students read Tanya's and Juan's stories. Then have them respond to the questions below either in small groups or as a class. Tell students that in their answers they should refer to personal experiences along with the information in the two vignettes. Point out that though there are no right or wrong answers to these questions, students should think critically and offer logical, thoughtful responses.

Responding to the Selection

1. What do you think the outcome of Tanya's story would have been if students from her school had *not* volunteered to help Mr. Dworkin?

2. What other jobs are needed to feed the homeless besides Juan's chores of picking up and delivering the food?

3. What kind of slogan would you use to enlist volunteers and to collect supplies for a homeless shelter? Describe or draw what you would use with the slogan.

ESL/LEP Strategy

Have ESL/LEP students suggest slogans that would elicit volunteer help from speakers of their native languages.

Ask ESL/LEP students if slogans created by the class for the previous activity can be translated directly into their native languages. Chances are most of the slogans do not translate easily. You may wish to point out that slogans often employ idioms and implied meanings that do not carry from one language to another.

Encourage ESL/LEP students to describe any idioms in the slogans they write and to translate the slogans into English as best as possible. You might also use students' slogans as examples of idioms.

Making New Friends (page 84)

Have students read this selection. You may wish to have students read the vignette silently or aloud.

Give the class an opportunity to discuss the story briefly. Then have each student write one letter from the list below. Tell them to take the point of view of one of the following people. Suggest that they use the pronouns *I* and *you* and details from the selection. They may also invent names, addresses, and other details, and may build on the story plot.

- A thank-you note to Douglas for his volunteer work from the director of the nursing home

- A card with a special message from Douglas to Mel on his ninety-first birthday

- An open letter to the high school volunteers in the Elder Care program from the staff and residents at the nursing home

- A newsletter published by the Elder Care program, in which they report on the services they are providing, invite others to become volunteers, and give recognition to special volunteers

Cooperative Learning Strategy

Divide students into three groups. Assign each group a person from the vignettes: Tanya, Juan, or Douglas. Tell each group to make a chart for one of these people. The chart will depict how the person benefited from volunteering and how others benefited from that person's service.

Have each group write the person's name at the top of the chart and make two columns under the name. On the top of the left column, students should write "Gave." On the top of the right column, they should write "Got."

Tell groups to brainstorm ways the volunteer helped others and to list them in the "Gave" column. Then have them brainstorm ways the volunteer

benefited from the experience. Tell groups to list those benefits in the "Got" column. Explain that they should get information from the volunteer's story, but that they may also infer some services and benefits.

When groups have finished, have them present their charts to the class. Invite class members to suggest anything else that might be added to each chart.

Thinking Strategy

Explain that critical thinkers often make inferences based on what they already know. Tell students that when critical thinkers infer, they conclude that something is true, based on facts and assumptions. For example, if it is dark outside, it is probably night.

Explain that critical thinkers remember, however, that even the best inferences are based on assumptions. If the assumption is incorrect, the inference will be incorrect. For example, if it is dark outside, it may not be night. Perhaps it is really noon, but a storm is brewing.

TEACHING THE LESSONS

Lesson 1: Examining Issues and Weighing Ideas (pages 85–87)

Thinking Skill Objectives:

- Students will **examine** social problems.
- Students will **weigh** and **assess** different options.
- Students will **decide** which kinds of volunteer work would suit them best.

Content Objective:

- Students will learn the importance of volunteer work.

After students have read the unit introduction, have them brainstorm reasons for volunteering. You may wish to have them brainstorm individually or in groups. Explain that there is nothing wrong with including benefits to the volunteers in the list of reasons for volunteering.

Sidenote Connection

When students have listed possible reasons for volunteering, ask them to compare what they wrote with the information in the "Why Volunteer?" sidenote on page 86.

Then suggest that students read the "Current Social Issues" sidenote before they begin filling in the "Volunteer Self-Questionnaire" on pages 85–86. Explain that the information in that sidenote might be especially helpful if they do not already have an idea for the volunteer activity they might want to do.

Cooperative Learning Strategy

After students have completed their self-questionnaires, you may wish to divide them into pairs for this cooperative learning activity.

Tell students that they will take turns role-playing interviewer and interviewee in a volunteer placement program. You may want to explain first that some larger volunteer organizations interview prospective volunteers to help them find their niche in the organization. Interviewers want to place the volunteer in a situation that will make the most of the person's talents and skills.

Suggest that the person playing the part of the interviewer look over the prospective volunteer's questionnaire and ask thoughtful, probing questions about the applicant's responses. Explain that the interviewer should get a clearer picture of the best placement for the volunteer during the interview.

You may wish to start interviews by giving students this example of the kinds of questions to ask: "I see that on your questionnaire you listed cooking both as something you do well and as something you enjoy doing. What kinds of foods do you most often make? Do you think you would like to help cook meals at one of our shelters?"

When each student has had a chance to play each role, encourage several pairs to perform their interviews for the class.

Thinking Journal

Ask students to write in their Thinking Journal about what they learned from taking the role of the interviewer. Tell them to think about the kinds of questions they asked and how they might use this information when they are interviewed for a volunteer position or program in the future.

Thinking Strategy

Explain to students that the process of inquiry, or one of generating questions, is a tool critical thinkers use to help each other explore inner thoughts and feelings.

What Works

Many teachers have found that they are more successful teaching thinking strategies to students when they offer students an opportunity to examine and reflect on their responses to questions.

Using the Graphic Organizer (page 87)

Explain to students that their answers will be based on their own opinions, preferences, and skills and will most likely be different from their classmates' answers.

You might have students share their responses and ask students to explain them, as well.

ESL/LEP Strategy

Have ESL/LEP students share information about volunteer programs, sponsors, and practices in their native countries with the class. Encourage the rest of the class to ask questions that compare and contrast volunteer work in other countries with volunteering in the United States.

Discussion (page 87)

Ask students why volunteer work is important. Then have them discuss the benefits of volunteer work for those being served and for the volunteers themselves.

When students seem to have touched on all the main benefits, discuss what students would say to people who do not think they have time for

What Works

Many teachers have found that structured discussions refine students' listening skills, increase their problem-solving skills, boost their self-esteem, and prepare them for on-the-job communication experiences.

volunteer work. Encourage students to use the benefits they mentioned previously as reasons for finding time to volunteer. Also recommend that they include in their arguments suggestions for how to budget one's time to make room for volunteer work.

Thinking Strategy

Explain to students that critical thinkers listen attentively and take notes during discussions. They add new information to their bank of knowledge, confirm inferences they have made, and raise new questions. Critical thinkers also ask clarifying questions during discussions.

Evaluation Tip

Consider evaluating and grading students on the Discussion and/or Alternative to the Discussion at the end of this lesson. Both activities serve as a means of summarizing, verbally or in writing, what students learned in the lesson. You might want to give the students specific criteria you will use for grading.

Lesson 2: Researching Community Needs (pages 88–89)

Thinking Skill Objectives:

- Students will **research** community volunteer opportunities.
- Students will **identify** places, things, or people that may need help.
- Students will **generate** questions and **interview** experts.
- Students will **gather information** on community needs.

Content Objective:

- Students will learn about the needs in their community.

Have students read the first paragraph on page 88. Then tell them to list places, things, or people that may need help. Explain that students may add more lines if necessary.

Advise students to use the Volunteer Resource Center they started at the beginning of this unit. Suggest that they browse through the center to gather information and donate information they collect from other sources.

Next, have students write their lists of contact people. Tell them not to forget relatives, friends, and acquaintances who are active in community affairs.

Tell them to base their interviews on the model on page 89, but remind them to keep their interviews fresh and original. Memorizing or reading a script will only produce a canned effect.

Advise students to use these guidelines in their telephone interviews:

1. Keep your tone of voice light and friendly.
2. If the person seems busy or preoccupied, ask when you may call back.
3. Listen carefully and ask follow-up questions to clarify information you do not immediately understand.

Encourage students to alphabetize by last name contacts they record in their logs. Suggest that groups post their lists of community volunteer job opportunities in the Volunteer Resource Center.

What Works

Many teachers have found that encouraging students to be "information pack rats" is to everyone's advantage. The contents of vehicles, such as a class Volunteer Resource Center, for example, need not be discarded at the end of a project. The files could be donated to the school library or kept in storage for future classes to peruse.

Thinking Skills

Explain to students that critical thinkers often log information they gather even though it may not seem pertinent to their needs at that time. It may turn out that the information they logged can be useful on another project, or it may be valuable to someone working on a similar task.

Sidenote Connection

Have students read the "Bookshelf" sidenote. Tell them to look up volunteering in the subject file of their library's card catalog or computer database. Ask them to list in the classroom Volunteer Resource Center books that they find particularly interesting. You may want to recommend the following books:

- *Care and Share: Teenagers and Volunteerism,* by Kathlyn Gau.
- *The Peace Corps Today,* by Merni Ingrassia Fitzgerald.

Have students also read the "Helpful Agencies" sidenote on page 88. You may wish to have the class compose a letter that can be sent to both agencies. Appoint a class secretary to take their dictation and draft the letter. Have the secretary read responses that are received from the agencies.

Cooperative Learning Strategy

Have students conduct mock interviews with contact people before they make actual calls. Divide groups into pairs. Tell partners to choose who will be an interviewer and who will be an interviewee. As each mock interview is being performed, the rest of the group may serve as the audience.

You may wish to allow groups to tape the mock interviews to play back for the class. Invite students to critique interview questions and to comment on various telephone techniques.

Evaluation Tip

After you have graded students' work in this lesson, using their participation in interviews and in gathering information as criteria, consider allowing students to evaluate their own work as well.

Have students compare the grade they gave themselves with the one you assigned. If there are discrepancies between the two grades, you may wish to hold conferences to discuss the differences.

Lesson 3: Evaluating Volunteer Opportunities (pages 90–91)

Thinking Skill Objectives:

- Students will **rank** options.
- Students will **examine** their job ideas.
- Students will **evaluate** volunteer opportunities.

Content Objective:

- Students will use their evaluations to recommend volunteer projects.

Have students read the unit introduction. You may wish to have students return to their groups from Lesson 2 as they complete the checklist on page 90 and rank the volunteer opportunities.

Suggest to students that they include in their list of issues anything that interested them in the Volunteer Resource Center.

Using the Graphic Organizer (page 91)

Suggest that students read the sidenote "Where Are the Volunteer Jobs?" on page 90 before they begin using the graphic organizer.

Tell students that they may add extra spokes and lines if they have more ideas than can fit on the chart. Invite one or more groups to copy their chart on the chalkboard and discuss it with the class.

What Works

Many teachers have found that a web-type graphic organizer can help students organize their thinking in three ways.

1. It helps them collect information.
2. It helps them generate new ideas.
3. It helps them assemble information and ideas into usable groupings.

Cooperative Learning Strategy

The following activity is designed to help students better understand what tasks are involved in various volunteer jobs and to help them visualize themselves doing the jobs they have listed. Students may remain in the groups that were formed for the graphic organizer activity.

Have each student choose one volunteer job from the ideas that have been generated. Tell students that they will imagine that they have just returned from doing their volunteer job and will now tell group members about their experiences.

Give students time to outline what they will say before their group. Tell them to include likely details about the day's tasks and events in the volunteer job they have selected. Ideas for details can be found in the "Where Are the Volunteer Jobs?" sidenote.

Suggest that groups get members to tell about their jobs by asking a question, such as "How did your day go, Sonya?" or "What did you do today, Roberto?"

Sidenote Connection

Before students recommend a volunteer project, have them read the sidenote "The Language of Thinking." Remind them to use the five criteria at the bottom of page 91, as they make their choice.

Thinking Strategy

Explain to students that critical thinkers often ask themselves questions such as the following when they make evaluations:

1. Am I clear about what it is that I am evaluating?
2. Do I know what my purpose is for evaluating?
3. Do I have specific criteria for evaluation that are relevant to my purpose?
4. Do I have enough information about what I am evaluating?
5. Are my criteria based on the information that I have?

ESL/LEP Strategy

You may wish at this point to have ESL/LEP students conduct a self-evaluation of how their participation in class activities and discussions has improved their English proficiency. Suggest that they use the following questions as part of their self-evaluation:

1. Am I using English in the classroom more often than I did at the beginning of the course?
2. Am I carrying over what I have learned in this class to conversations, reading, and writing outside the classroom?
3. Do I feel that I have a better understanding of figures of speech, idioms, and other forms of expression?

Consider having ESL/LEP students give you both a written self-evaluation and an oral assessment of their progress in English proficiency. They might also be encouraged to suggest areas that could be improved.

Evaluation Tip

In addition to evaluating students' written work (lists, charts, notes), you may wish to use the following questions as part of your criteria when assigning grades for this lesson:

- Did the student voluntarily participate in class discussions and activities?
- How often and in what kinds of activities did he or she participate?
- Did the student give carefully thought out and fully developed responses or only "yes" and "no" answers?
- Did the student contribute materials to the class Volunteer Resource Center?

MAKING CONNECTIONS

Starting a Volunteer Project (pages 92–95)

Thinking Skill Objectives:

- Students will **plan** and **organize** a group volunteer project.
- Students will **formulate** a purpose for the project.
- Students will **evaluate** their projects.

Content Objectives:

- Students will make commitments to volunteer activities.
- Students will put their project into action.
- Students will publicize their work in newspapers and other media.

Have students read the project introduction on page 92. As you discuss the project with students, ask how they might apply to it what they have learned in this unit and in previous units.

Step 1: Making a Personal Commitment (pages 92–93)

As a first step in their projects, students should form groups of three or four members and choose a volunteer project. They will then complete their commitment checklists and discuss the kinds of commitments they are able to make to a volunteer job. Allow students who do not feel capable of making the same commitments as the others in the group to change groups.

It is important that students not feel guilty if they cannot volunteer much time to projects. Some students may have part-time jobs, and others may be responsible for the care of younger children. Encourage each student to participate in whatever way they can.

Thinking Strategy

Tell students that making a commitment to a volunteer project poses a multidimensional problem. Explain that a multidimensional problem is one that can be analyzed and approached from several viewpoints. Explain that critical thinkers are multilogical thinkers, and they try to analyze multidimensional problems from several points of view. Advise students to analyze their answers on the checklist in multilogical ways to see if their goals are realistic.

What Works

Many teachers find great value in having students use multilogical thinking to analyze the commitments that need to be made before joining an ongoing project that will need their continuing participation. Multilogical thinking encourages the individual to see a situation from the points of view of the many "hats" he or she wears: student, family member, team or club member, employee. Multilogical thinking usually involves sorting through the various responsibilities and schedules that are "worn" with each hat.

Step 2: Organizing a Group (pages 93–94)

Have students begin this step by finding advisers, sponsors, and consultants. Offer yourself as an adviser only if a group has repeatedly tried and failed to find someone else.

You may wish to suggest that groups display their statement of purpose on a poster or banner in their "headquarters," which may be the section of the classroom where their group meets.

Along with their statement of purpose, which answers the question "Why do we want to do this job?", they may wish to display a "Jobs To Do" sheet. You may wish to appoint students to check that every member of the group is accounted for on the list-of-tasks sheet, and that individuals are completing their tasks. Advise the person responsible for each set of tasks to put the initials of the person who did it next to each completed job.

Cooperative Learning Strategy

If students need funding for their projects, you may want to help them launch a direct-mail campaign to elicit donations.

Have representatives from each group check with your municipality to find out what kinds of permits they may need for fund raising or any other aspects of their projects.

Other group members may take responsibility for writing letters to the editors of local newspapers to announce their projects and to request financial support.

Each group should have a treasurer to keep track of incoming and outgoing money, although you may wish to keep the money in a class or school bank account. (Keeping large amounts of money in the classroom is not advisable.)

The member of each group who receives funds should be responsible for writing thank you letters to contributors.

You may wish to use the following strategy for selecting members responsible for each letter-writing task. Have every member in the group count off, starting at one. Pick a random number from 1 to 4 and have each student with that number assume the letter-writing job named.

ESL/LEP Strategy

Encourage ESL/LEP students to act as liaisons with the non-English speaking community. Even if they do not speak the same language as most other non-English speakers in the area, ESL/LEP students will be more aware of where bilingual aid may be needed. Are bilingual signs needed in homeless shelters? Do some elderly people not understand how to take medications because they can't read English? Perhaps some non-English-speaking preschoolers who will soon enter kindergarten need help with basic English words.

Step 3: Taking Action (page 95)

Have students read "A Beach Cleanup," then have each group discuss the story. You may want to have students use the following questions as discussion starters.

1. How is your project different from the one in "A Beach Cleanup." How are the projects similar?

2. How did the students get started on their project?

3. What might be the best way to get your project started?

Step 4: Publicizing Your Experiences (page 95)

Consider setting aside a certain time and day of the week for students to meet and report on their experiences. You may wish to appoint Friday afternoons, for example, as report time.

Local media are usually eager to report upbeat citizen-aid stories. Make sure groups contact television and radio stations, as well as local newspapers, whenever something of particular interest happens or when supplies or funds may be needed.

Also suggest that groups create books about their projects. The books may include diary entries; vignettes similar to those of Tanya, Juan, and Douglas in the opening of this unit; or letters to and from people involved in the project. Encourage students to include photographs and drawings in their books and to add a table of contents and an index.

Before putting covers on the books (binders or folders would work well), photocopy the pages so that every student may have a copy. Make a few extra copies for the classroom Volunteer Resource Center, the library, and for sponsors. Encourage groups to read and discuss each others' books.

If groups have access to video recorders, you may suggest that they make documentaries about their volunteer work. A documentary could recount how the project was begun, show the need for and the purpose of the work, and report on what the group has accomplished.

You may wish to advise students who are interested in making documentaries to first view documentary films available at libraries and video stores in order to familiarize themselves with the form.

Thinking Strategy

Explain to students that some critical thinkers have found the documentary to be an effective vehicle for analyzing and reflecting on an event, era, or situation, and for communicating their thoughts about the subject to others.

Step 5: Evaluating Your Project (page 95)

Advise students to make a chart that they can use at their regular group meetings to evaluate the progress of their volunteer projects.

Suggest that they adapt the questions in this step for use on the chart. Tell students to add as many questions as they need.

Each question could be written in a column on the left side of the chart, and a grid that allows for check marks could fill the right side. By photocopying the chart, groups could have a fresh form to use at each meeting.

Suggest that students use two different colored markers to complete the charts. A green check could mean that a facet of the project is progressing well. A red mark would point out an aspect that needs attention. If a question receives a red mark two meetings in a row, the problem should be carefully looked into by the group.

Thinking Journal

Students might write a self-evaluation of their project in their Thinking Journals. Tell them to describe the thinking skills and strategies they used to plan and complete their projects.

Unit Test (page 96)

In addition to, or as an alternative to, the unit project, you may wish to have students complete the unit test.

Responses

1. b. Students may refer to President Kennedy's appeal for volunteerism.

2. True, true, false. Critical thinkers find that amassing a list of options and evaluating all of them helps them to make reasoned decisions. They also use their own experiences to inform their choices.

3. Answers will vary. Students should mention various aspects of their daily lives and how the thinking skills and strategies they have learned will help them make choices.

4. Answers will vary. Students should state whether they agree or disagree that urban violence reflects the community. They should then support their argument with reasons, details, and examples.

Getting Started as a Teacher of Critical Thinking

What does it mean to be a teacher of critical thinking? How, practically speaking, does a teacher maintain responsibility for teaching and turn over responsibility for learning to students? How is it possible to improve a student's thinking processes? What does being a teacher of critical thinking mean in terms of everyday interactions with students and how you manage the classroom? How do you have to change to be a good teacher of critical thinking?

These are only a few of the questions asked by teachers who confront the challenge of teaching critical thinking skills for the first time. Perhaps the large question behind them all is, "What does a critical thinking teacher look and act like?" In fact, successful teachers of critical thinking share certain characteristics, particularly in teaching style and methodology. An effective teacher of critical thinking:

- creates an environment that encourages good thinking.
- sets clear goals, objectives, and purposes.
- uses the language of thinking.
- models thinking and metacognition, or thinking about thinking.
- asks questions and makes comments that show respect for students' thinking.
- allows time for discussion and thoughtful deliberation.
- uses cooperative learning groups.

Making a Commitment

Critical thinking theorists suggest that before you begin any critical thinking program you may need to explain to students that they will be engaged in a different type of teaching-learning system than they have been used to. The reason for this difference is that, to become independent critical thinkers, they must take an active role in their own learning.

Students engage in discussions, debates, and activities where they express themselves openly. They share their ideas, as well as the process they used to get those ideas. They listen to others' ideas and weigh them in terms of criteria that are agreed on and understood. They work on activities independently or in cooperative groups where they collaborate with others and take some responsibility for the whole group's success.

To be successful, teachers and students have to commit to the long-term goal of self-education and self-motivation.

Creating a Positive Environment

A teacher of critical thinking has the job of providing a supportive, trusting, and calm environment in which students feel safe sharing their thoughts and ideas. To achieve such an environment, students need ground rules. Students can collaborate to develop the rules, for example:

- Anyone who is talking can finish without being interrupted.
- Everyone will share ideas with the group or class.
- Every students' ideas will be acknowledged and considered.
- All comments will be positive and helpful.

Post them in a place where everyone can see them.

Setting Clear Goals and Purpose

Students need to know what is expected of them and what they can expect from the teacher and the program. There should be a clear purpose for the tasks students are asked to do, and the tasks should be relevant to students' lives. Sometimes you might ask students to articulate the purpose and relevancy of an assignment or activity. To determine whether students understand the purpose and objective of a task, ask them to restate those elements in their own words. When they understand the purpose and appropriateness of activities, students take more responsibility for their success.

Using the Language of Thinking

Teachers of critical thinking need to use the language of thinking in their daily lessons. Students of critical thinking need to hear and to understand the names of the skills and processes they are learning, practicing, and applying. For example, students should be required to name the skills they are applying, such as evaluation, identification, application, and so on. As it is part of the normal class activities, the language of thinking quickly becomes part of students' language.

Students need to know that thinking is not something accomplished by only a select few people, but rather that it is something that everyone does all the time. Students also need to know that no one ever completely masters the art of thinking, but rather that everyone gets better with practice and feedback. They need to know that there are ways to tell how they are doing and that they will participate in evaluating their progress.

Modeling Metacognitive Processes

Students need to hear how other people arrive at ideas or conclusions. By listening to others describe how they think, students can learn new ways to evaluate and process information. Initially, the burden of modeling metacognition rests on the teacher. By thinking aloud and talking about thinking, a teacher can show students the process.

Students benefit from repeated practice in describing their own processes by listening to a teacher's models and by observing other students' attempts. It is also useful to have students record their thinking processes and those of others in a journal. These descriptions serve not only as a reminder for later use but also as a record of the student's progress.

Asking Questions

In a supportive learning environment, teachers ask questions and make comments that show appreciation and respect for a diversity of opinions. A goal of teachers of critical thinking is to have students carry on thoughtful discussions without teacher management or intervention. Students should be aware of this goal so that they can work toward assuming this responsibility.

Asking good questions requires practice. Questions such as the following are intended to generate discussion and encourage feedback. Over time, teachers can train students to ask these kinds of questions of their classmates and of themselves.

1. I'm interested in your opinion. Why do you believe that?
2. What kind of evidence can you give to support that opinion?
3. I'm trying to visualize your idea. Describe it in a different way to help me see it better.
4. What experiences have you had that make you draw that conclusion?
5. How could you describe that idea to someone who has not had your experiences?
6. What possible solutions are we missing?
7. On a scale of 1–10, how would you rank that solution for its long-lasting effect?
8. How accurate do you think your assumptions are?
9. I'm having trouble with this argument. Help me follow your logic.
10. Where could you go to find reliable information about this topic?

Encouraging Thoughtful Discussion

An important element teachers of critical thinking use in discussions is wait time, or the time a student has before the correct answer is given or another student is given the opportunity to answer. Teachers of critical thinking know that when students are given wait time there is a perceptible increase in the creativity, appropriateness, and thinking behind their responses.

Art Costa, one of the foremost staff developers in critical thinking, states, "When [you] ask a question and then wait for a student's answer, it demonstrates that [you] not only expect an answer but also that [you] have faith in the student's ability to answer it given enough time. If [you] ask a question and then wait only a short time, then give the answer for [the student], call on another student, give a hint, or seek help from another student, it demonstrates that the student really can't answer the question and is considered too poor a student to offer an answer or to be able to reason for him/herself."

Using Cooperative Learning Strategies

Establishing and using cooperative learning groups is also an effective technique for teaching critical thinking. Students in groups can generate more ideas than individuals can. Also, students learn from one another and gain confidence as they share ideas and thinking strategies in small, supportive groups before presenting them to the class.

Becoming an effective teacher of critical thinking does not happen overnight. It requires changes in teaching behaviors that come only with patience and practice. The first step in getting started is making a commitment to change. With that commitment, you and your students can create an environment that fosters the learning and application of creative, analytical, and critical thinking.

Teaching Critical Thinking in a Multicultural Classroom

No one would challenge that the need for critical thinking is universal. Certainly the benefits of clear and effective thinking cross all cultures and ethnic groups. But there are some differences among student populations that teachers need to recognize and accommodate to be effective in a multicultural setting.

How can the content of a thinking program accommodate a diverse student population? How can teachers accommodate different thinking and learning styles in a classroom? And how can teachers promote English-language acquisition though thinking skills instruction? By understanding how students process information, by observing how they respond to teacher prompts, and by ascertaining what issues they consider valuable, teachers can modify instruction in appropriate and effective ways.

The Importance of Topical Content

The content in *Thinking It Through* was selected with a two-fold purpose in mind. First, the topics were chosen because they are relevant for all young people in today's society. They focus on issues that all teens deal with in their daily lives. Second, the topics in *Thinking It Through* reflect common issues and influences in American culture. By examining and reflecting on issues in American society, students from other cultures can come to understand them without being unduly influenced by them. Critical thinking instruction and practice around these issues can promote thoughtful acculturation.

Teachers should become familiar both with the local issues that affect or involve diverse groups, as well as with resources that present those issues fully and objectively. Then these issues or topics can be incorporated into daily lessons. By using this strategy, students from all cultures can become more informed and open-minded about the concerns of diverse groups in the community.

Strategies for Accommodating Diverse Thinking/Response Styles

One important goal and benefit of thinking skill instruction is to develop an appreciation of one's own thinking behavior, style, and processes. A corollary goal is to observe and develop an appreciation of how others think and communicate their thinking. Some-times as students from other cultures observe how students from the majority culture behave they may perceive their own thinking and learning styles to be less worthy. By helping students clarify their thinking processes, by modeling metacognition, by discussing thinking strategies, and by encouraging students to observe everyone's thinking processes, teachers can promote open-mindedness and an appreciation for diversity in thinking and response styles.

Adjust the pace. A goal of critical thinking instruction is to control impulsive responses and to promote reflective thinking. However, sometimes, in classroom practice, students who give speedy and facile responses appear to be the brightest students. Students who take time to deliberate about their responses may be perceived by other students, or more significantly, may perceive themselves, as slower or less able.

Students from some ethnic groups may value deliberation, recognizing that good judgments take time. For all students, the pace of instruction should be varied, and all students should be encouraged to take time for reflection. For ethnically diverse students, it is especially important to acknowledge and reinforce their careful thinking, affirming that deliberation is a valued trait.

Use a variety of modalities. Often students from diverse cultures appreciate different thinking and learning modalities. Some value oral discourse; others value writing. Some prefer to process information visually; others favor hands-on learning. The activities in *Thinking It Through* include graphic organizers for the visual learner, journals for students who reinforce their thinking by writing, and discussion for oral learners. Despite any preferred learning styles, all students benefit from a variety of techniques and modalities. However, to make critical thinking instruction most effective and meaningful, it is important to be alert to individual preferences and to accommodate those insofar as possible.

Recognize behavioral values. It is important for teachers to become familiar with the diverse values from students' cultures and to consider those values during daily lessons to improve and promote students' learning. For example, persistence is a highly valued behavior in some cultures. If teachers identify students to whom persistence is important, they can be cautious about cutting short activities or discussions before students' persistence pays off.

Some cultural values may be threatened by the very nature of important critical thinking strategies.

For example, respect for the authority of the teacher is a value in many cultures. This respect may lead some students to believe that the teacher will accept only one right answer and that they must figure out the answer. Also, in many cultures, adults do not routinely explain their thinking to teenagers. As a result, when students hear teachers thinking aloud and modeling metacognition, they may feel awkward or suspect that their thinking, if different, is wrong. Over time, and with repeated encouragement of differences in responses and styles, teachers can help students become more self-confident.

Reinforce unique language behaviors. Some students may come from cultures that have a strong oral history tradition. In such cultures, rhyme and repetition are often used to emphasize points and to aid retention. Teachers can take advantage of such linguistic-cultural devices to aid students' learning and thinking. For example, if teachers recognize the idioms, rhythms, and styles of speaking among students, they can employ similar techniques to help students remember words, concepts, and thinking processes.

Become sensitive to gender issues. In some cultures, young people are reluctant to discuss their ideas in mixed-gender classes. To encourage necessary openness, teachers can organize single-gender cooperative learning groups. In this way, male and female students can become more comfortable expressing their ideas because they rehearse in small, comfortable groups before participating in whole-class discussions.

Strategies for Encouraging English Language Development

Critical thinking encourages language acquisition in two ways: (1) the expanded grammar and vocabulary resulting from activities where students seek reasons, details, and examples that support critical judgments and (2) the language of thinking resulting from metacognitive activities where students describe their thinking.

Since the vocabulary of thinking seems more abstract than day-to-day English dialogue, teachers are sometimes reluctant to use or expect students to use vocabulary related to metacognition. Teachers who have taught critical thinking to ESL/LEP students have found that students pick up metacognitive language easily and learn to use it as precisely and as easily as they learn any other vocabulary.

Have student keep journals. Keeping journals or portfolios that track the development of one's own thinking is helpful for all students. However, for ESL/LEP students who are shy about speaking in class, journals can be especially important confidence-builders as they bear witness to students' own growth.

Encourage whole-sentence responses. Often ESL/LEP students hear only the English conversation of friends or family, which may be non-standard or expressed only in phrases or sentence fragments. ESL/LEP students may also have poor language development in their native language and may not speak using whole sentences. Teachers can model desirable language behaviors by using whole-sentence directions and responses with students. In turn, teachers can accept from students only whole-sentence responses and explain why saying, for example, "Your thought is a good one and I want to understand it correctly, so tell me your idea in a complete statement."

Require writing in every lesson. Writing can be the "hard copy" of thinking, both the outcome and the expression of thought. Whether for their own use or for the teacher's review, students should be constantly encouraged to write. Students' writing should be of two kinds: (1) responses or ideas about topics and issues, and (2) descriptions of, or reflections on, their own thinking processes.

Use computer technology. Some students may be comfortable or experienced with electronic media in their own culture. Teachers can set up electronic mail networks if the classroom or school has the equipment. ESL/LEP students can discuss lesson issues with proficient English speakers via computer networks or electronic mail systems. Also, students can be encouraged to use computers for their writing, making use of editing systems to help with their spelling, vocabulary, and grammar.

To accomplish these goals in any program requires that teachers get to know their students. The activities in *Thinking It Through* provide teachers with a practical means to observe how their students process information to distinguish the issues and topics they value and to identify the learning styles they prefer. This information, acquired through the program lessons, allows teachers to make choices about practice and to modify their instruction as it takes place so that all students can perform to their highest potential and achieve success.

Assessing Critical Thinking

A former mayor of New York City used to ask his constituents periodically, "How am I doing?" We assume from his question that he wanted an honest assessment of his performance as mayor. A thoughtful response to the question called for citizens to think critically about what His Honor did well and what areas of his performance needed improvement. Of course, the final judgment of the mayor's performance happened on election day.

Students of critical thinking have the same question, "How am I doing?" They need an assessment of their abilities to think: to reason, analyze, predict, estimate, solve problems, and so on. They want an evaluation of their abilities to apply higher-order thinking skills in learning situations. And, equally importantly, they need to know if they are growing as critical thinkers. For students, the most meaningful evaluation would not be as black and white as the mayor's election results. Numerical or letter grades alone should not be the only judgment of a student's performance. To continue to improve their use of higher-order thinking skills, students need more helpful and authentic measurements of their abilities.

What Is Authentic Assessment?

For students to develop critical thinking skills they need to be involved in thought-provoking, real-world activities that call for them to think, act, and communicate. Activities need to challenge learners to analyze, synthesize, apply, and evaluate information in a variety of contexts, including some of their own choosing.

To evaluate students' critical thinking skills, the same contexts must exist. Any assessment—whether by teachers or by students themselves—should be an integral part of learning and of the activities and assignments students are given. Evaluation criteria must be consistent, relevant, and appropriate to the assessment of higher-order thinking.

The activities in *Thinking It Through* provide opportunities for both the development and the evaluation of students' critical thinking skills. To help students monitor and assess their own growth, you may ask them to maintain Thinking Journals, to conduct peer reviews, and to develop simple criteria for project and test evaluation.

Thinking Journals

Thinking Journals provide students with a format for tracking their critical thinking through reflective writing. As they read selections, discuss issues, complete exercises, plan projects, or conduct research, they can use their journals to record experiences, to list and weigh possibilities, to reflect or comment on issues, to note connections, or to describe metacognitive strategies they use. *Thinking It Through* provides suggestions for Thinking Journal entries in the TRM. In addition, there is a reproducible master for a Thinking Journal on page 62 of the TRM. Journal writing can stimulate constructive thinking. In time, students will regard reflective writing as a useful way of recording and commenting on their own learning.

Thinking Journals also offer students a forum for evaluating their contributions to group projects, as well as their performance on independent activities. The questions in the "Evaluation" boxes in each lesson of *Thinking It Through* are constructed to stimulate students' reflections and evaluations and, therefore, can become a part of students' Thinking Journals. The evaluation questions ask students to examine their own learning processes and to target specific areas for improvement. The answers to the questions provide students and teachers with a rationale for evaluation. Both the nature and the purpose of the self-evaluation questions combine to make assessment authentic.

Thinking Journals also promote the development of higher-order thinking skills as they engage students in the process of using language in realistic contexts. As students regularly put their ideas, impressions, and self-assessments into writing, they gain greater discipline and fluency with written language, as well as more logic in their thinking.

Peer Reviews

As students become more effective language users, they learn to think more critically. Therefore, students need rich and varied contexts—reading, writing, speaking, and listening—within which they can use language and think critically. Peer reviews offer an opportunity for even the most reluctant students to try out language in all its forms for the development of higher-order thinking skills. As students review their work with each other in small groups, they collaborate to improve each other's work—both in communicating ideas and in employing thinking processes.

Successful peer reviews require planning and practice. *Thinking It Through* provides many opportunities for teachers to structure peer reviews. For example, students are frequently called upon to evaluate group projects. As they use criteria for measuring the success of their own and others' work, students practice analyzing and evaluating information in regular, authentic contexts.

As students work together to assess and evaluate their own and their peers' skills as critical thinkers, students gain confidence in making decisions and synthesizing information. They develop proficiency in using language, which is integral to both learning and constructive thinking.

Prepared Tests

It is true that students learn what the teacher tests, but teachers know that the way in which learning is tested often determines the nature of the learning. Traditional objective tests usually measure students' abilities to recall information within specific contexts. To assess critical thinking skills, tests must be designed to measure more complex tasks, such as reasoning for understanding, making inferences, and solving problems. Most traditional tests are not authentic for this purpose.

Multiple choice items, true/false statements, and short-answer questions can be appropriate evaluation formats so long as they provide students with opportunities to make and explain judgments. The validity of such tests is greatly increased as students are required to explain their answers. The tests in *Thinking It Through* give students opportunities both to formulate answers to provocative questions and to explain their choices or responses. The authenticity of the tests in *Thinking It Through* lies in the latter aspect of this important dual function.

Using Criteria for Assessment

Clearly stated, straightforward criteria describe the basis on which students' work will be judged. These criteria may be developed by the teacher, by students, or by a collaboration. For example, teachers and students may work together to list the appropriate attributes to consider when evaluating a debate, essay, or opinion paper. Those attributes could include:

- **Content:** quality and accuracy of reasons, examples and details, fair statement of opposing views
- **Development:** statement of subject to be discussed, clearly defined position, reason(s), appropriate and sufficient number of examples and details to support the reason(s)
- **Organization:** logical progression of the argument to a reasonable conclusion
- **Style:** appropriate number of paragraphs, attention to language mechanics

Once the important attributes of the assignments have been determined, both the teacher and students can judge a work in terms of how well it exemplifies the agreed-upon attributes of content, development, organization, and style. By developing criteria, both can agree on the meaning of each grade. Students can also use the criteria as guidelines for completing assignments.

By using shared criteria to evaluate their own and others' work, students are practicing the application of critical thinking to real-life situations. Students see how evaluative reasoning is relevant and practical to their lives and how strategies for assessment and evaluation can serve as models of clear, logical thinking.

The goal of authentic assessment is to empower students with the critical thinking skills and strategies that prepare them to take responsibility for their own learning. Through authentic assessment formats, such as thinking journals, peer reviews, and prepared tests, students can answer their question, "How am I doing?"

THINKING JOURNAL:
Thinking about My Thinking

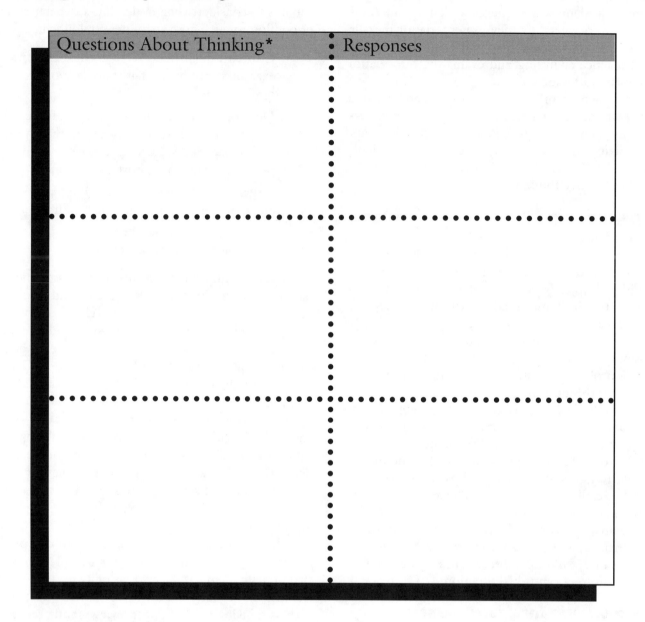

Questions About Thinking*	Responses

*Possible questions to reflect on my thinking

1. How did using a graphic organizer help me to organize my thinking?

2. Did I really defend my answer, conclusion, or opinion? How?

3. What steps did I use to arrive at my answer or conclusion?

4. Was the process I used to arrive at my answer or conclusion successful? Why or why not?

5. When can I use this thinking process again?

6. On a scale of 1 to 5 (5 being the highest), how would I evaluate the quality of my thinking on this task/assignment?

Glossary of Thinking Terms

• • • • • • • • • • • • • • • • • • •

To **analyze** means to break apart the whole into smaller parts in order to establish a pattern or relationship.

To **assess,** or to evaluate, means to judge the value or worth of something.

To **compare and contrast** means to find similarities in and differences between two or more things. When comparing or contrasting, you look at similar aspects of the two things. For example, in contrasing boats and ships, you could examine their size and function to find similarities and differences.

Decision making is a process by which people make choices. A simple way to make decisions is by following these steps:

1. State the issue or problem.
2. List possible actions or solutions.
3. Consider all of the options.
4. Weigh the pros and cons for each option.
5. Make the best choice.

Distinguishing requires you to recognize aspects of two or more ideas or objects so that you can tell them apart.

To **draw conclusions** means to combine information that you already have with new information that you receive. The result is a conclusion, an opinion, or a belief.

To **evaluate** means to judge or to determine the worth or value of something. Making evaluations requires careful thinking and weighing of all sides before forming an informed judgment.

To **examine** means to study something in all its parts, with a goal in mind.

To **inquire or question** means to ask questions about information you read, see, or hear in order to understand, clarify, or evaluate the validity of information.

Interpreting means to make an assessment or to give one's point of view.

When you **observe** something, you look at or watch it very carefully, paying special attention to details.

Planning is a very important life skill. It is a skill that involves many other skills. It involves thinking about the future while taking past experiences and present knowledge into account. It involves making predictions about future needs and actions. It also involves understanding actions and their consequences.

When **predicting**, critical thinkers use what they already know. They then consider the possibilities and probabilities of what might happen in the future.

To **prioritize** means to put in order of importance. Put the most important thing first, the next most important thing second, and so on.

To **read critically** means to analyze the meaning of a passage. It also requires you to ask questions about what you are reading either to clarify information or to evaluate it.

To **recognize** means to be able to identify an object or an idea.

Researching means identifying and using expert help to find information.

Tips for Learning English as a Second Language

 1. As you read, use a highlighter pen to highlight key words.

 2. Write new words that you read or hear on the front of index cards. Write definitions on the back of the cards. Review these cards often.

 3. Work with a partner who speaks English and your native language.

 4. In group discussions, act out words and concepts if you do not know the right words to use. Ask group members to help you find the right words.

 5. Use a bilingual dictionary whenever you need to.

 6. Use memory games to remember how to spell words. For example, to remember the difference between principal (the head of the school) and principle (a rule or regulation), think of the phrase: The princi**pal** is our **pal**.

 7. Do not be afraid to ask a student or the teacher to repeat or explain something that you do not understand.

 8. Tape record class lectures and discussions. Listen to them again at your own pace.

 9. Teach other students about your culture and values.

 10. When writing, do not worry about spelling and grammar in the first draft. On the second draft, use a dictionary to help you revise your work.